In the Beginning

In the Beginning

How It All Started

2nd Edition

Allison Dee Parkman, MD, MDiv

Contents

Acknowledgments

I first want to thank God for saving me and filling me with His Holy Spirit. He has given me a passion to teach. I thank my parents, Ronald and Valencia, for all they have done for me. I want to acknowledge all the church ministries that have taught and encouraged me: Macedonia Baptist Church (Akron, OH), First Apostolic Faith Church (Akron, OH), Bethel Apostolic Temple (Toledo, OH), and The Way of Holiness Ministries (Jackson, LA). And of course, I cannot forget to thank all of my students that I have taught over the years.

Introduction

I believe that understanding Genesis is crucial to understanding the rest of the Bible, the plan of salvation, and—most importantly—God. My goal is not to write an all-inclusive, in-depth commentary or theological study of the book of Genesis in the King James Version of the Bible. Instead, I hope to present some main points and themes from the book in a simple way so one can gain an understanding and appreciation for Genesis and how it ties into the rest of the Bible.

Most people, whether they are Christians or not, are familiar with the stories of Genesis. There are movies, plays, and musicals about many of the events in this book. Although most people are familiar with the stories of Genesis, they do not feel that Genesis applies to their lives.

Obviously, I believe Genesis is relevant to our lives today. Genesis answers many of the questions we often ask ourselves: Where did we come from? Where did the world come from? What is our purpose? Who is God? How should we relate to God?

Genesis is the first book of the Bible and is appropriately named because it means "beginning" or "origin."[1] Technically, Genesis's authorship is anonymous because the author does not identify himself. Although there has been recent debate about Genesis's authorship, traditionally Moses is considered the author.[2]

---

[1] Tremper Longman III, *How to Read Genesis* (Downers Grove: InterVarsity Press, 2005), 14.
[2] Ibid., 56.

Although Moses may be the human author, I believe that Genesis was written by divine inspiration from God.[3] The original audience was the Israelite people as they were traveling from Egypt to the land of Canaan. As we read Genesis, we must understand the language and events in the original context to understand their significance to us today.

Genesis is a book of theology. *Theology* simply means "the study of God."[4] Although there are some aspects of Genesis that could be categorized as scientific or anthropological, one must remember Genesis's primary purpose is theology. Genesis introduces us to God, reveals that He is the Creator of all things, and reveals His character. In Genesis, we learn how sin entered the world and God's plan of redemption by establishing a chosen people by which all humanity will be able to be saved.

Genesis is a narrative. The author not only knows the events but the thoughts of the characters. There are several prominent themes throughout Genesis, such as the promise of land, the promise of fruitfulness, and most importantly the promise of restoration. Some minor themes are the significance of Egypt, sibling rivalry, family favoritism, and infertility.

I am confident that as you read this book, you will gain an appreciation for the book of Genesis, a greater understanding of the Bible, learn more about God, and most of all grow closer to the only Lord and Savior, Jesus Christ.

Review
   1. Why is the book of Genesis important?
   2. What does Genesis mean?
   3. Who is the author of Genesis?
   4. What are some major and minor themes of Genesis?
   5. What aspects of Genesis fall into the categories of science, history, and anthropology?

---

[3] 2 Timothy 3:16
[4] Millard Erickson, *Christian Theology*, 3rd ed. (Grand Rapids: Baker Book House, 2013), 8.

Genesis Chapter 1

1 In the beginning God created the heaven and the earth.

2 And the earth was without form, and void; and darkness was upon the face of the deep. And the Spirit of God moved upon the face of the waters.

3 And God said, Let there be light: and there was light.

4 And God saw the light, that it was good: and God divided the light from the darkness.

5 And God called the light Day, and the darkness he called Night. And the evening and the morning were the first day.

6 And God said, Let there be a firmament in the midst of the waters, and let it divide the waters from the waters.

7 And God made the firmament, and divided the waters which were under the firmament from the waters which were above the firmament: and it was so.

8 And God called the firmament Heaven. And the evening and the morning were the second day.

9 And God said, Let the waters under the heaven be gathered together unto one place, and let the dry land appear: and it was so.

10 And God called the dry land Earth; and the gathering together of the waters called he Seas: and God saw that it was good.

11 And God said, Let the earth bring forth grass, the herb yielding seed, and the fruit tree yielding fruit after his kind, whose seed is in itself, upon the earth: and it was so.

12 And the earth brought forth grass, and herb yielding seed after his kind, and the tree yielding fruit, whose seed was in itself, after his kind: and God saw that it was good.

13 And the evening and the morning were the third day.

14 And God said, Let there be lights in the firmament of the heaven to divide the day from the night; and let them be for signs, and for seasons, and for days, and years:

15 And let them be for lights in the firmament of the heaven to give light upon the earth: and it was so.

16 And God made two great lights; the greater light to rule the day, and the lesser light to rule the night: he made the stars also.

17 And God set them in the firmament of the heaven to give light upon the earth,

18 And to rule over the day and over the night, and to divide the light from the darkness: and God saw that it was good.

19 And the evening and the morning were the fourth day.

20 And God said, Let the waters bring forth abundantly the moving creature that hath life, and fowl that may fly above the earth in the open firmament of heaven.

21 And God created great whales, and every living creature that moveth, which the waters brought forth abundantly, after their kind, and every winged fowl after his kind: and God saw that it was good.

22 And God blessed them, saying, Be fruitful, and multiply, and fill the waters in the seas, and let fowl multiply in the earth.

23 And the evening and the morning were the fifth day.

24 And God said, Let the earth bring forth the living creature after his kind, cattle, and creeping thing, and beast of the earth after his kind: and it was so.

25 And God made the beast of the earth after his kind, and cattle after their kind, and every thing that creepeth upon the earth after his kind: and God saw that it was good.

26 And God said, Let us make man in our image, after our likeness: and let them have dominion over the fish of the sea, and over the fowl of the air, and over the cattle, and over all the earth, and over every creeping thing that creepeth upon the earth.

27 So God created man in his own image, in the image of God created he him; male and female created he them.

28 And God blessed them, and God said unto them, Be fruitful, and multiply, and replenish the earth, and subdue it: and have dominion over the fish of the sea, and over the fowl of the air, and over every living thing that moveth upon the earth.

29 And God said, Behold, I have given you every herb bearing seed, which is upon the face of all the earth, and every tree, in the which is the fruit of a tree yielding seed; to you it shall be for meat.

30 And to every beast of the earth, and to every fowl of the air, and to every thing that creepeth upon the earth, wherein there is life, I have given herb for meat: and it was so.

31 And God saw every thing that he had made, and behold, it was very good. And the evening and the morning were the sixth day.

Summary

vv. 1–2

God identifies Himself as Creator and describes the state of the earth.

vv. 3–5

In the first day, God creates light and darkness. He also creates day and night.

vv. 6–8

God creates the heavens, also called the sky, on the second day.

vv. 9–13

God creates the land, sea, and plants, and he describes them as good on the third day.

vv. 14–19

On the fourth day, God creates the stars, the moon, and the sun, and he describes them as good.

vv. 20–23

On the fifth day, God makes the fish and the birds. He blesses them and commands them to be fruitful and multiply. He also states that they are good.

vv. 24–25

On the sixth day, God creates land, animals, and man. God commands them to reproduce after their own kind and states that they are good.

vv. 26–28

God makes man in His own image and likeness and gives them dominion over all living things and over all the earth. God creates both male and female in His own image. God blesses them and commands them to be fruitful and to multiply.

vv. 29–30

God states that he has given the plants as food for man, animals, and birds.

v. 31

God sees that everything He has made is very good, and that is the end of the sixth day.

Commentary

In the very first verse, God identifies Himself as Creator. Moses continues to describe the creation of more specific aspects of the earth and living beings. Although there is debate about whether the days stated in this chapter are twenty-four-hour time periods or longer periods of time,[5] Moses emphasizes that God created all things. Even the natural laws that we observe, such as gravity, were set in place by God.

God created the universe by speaking it into existence. God took nothing, or no substance, and created life from it. This is called *creatio ex nihilo*.[6] This is in contrast to when humans create something. As humans, we take a substance or something that already exists and make it into another object. We cannot take "nothing or no substance" and make life from it. Although the scientific community generally agrees with the theory of naturalistic evolution[7] and the big bang theory[8] to explain the existence of the universe, even they admit that these are just theories, and there is not enough scientific evidence to prove that these theories are correct. There is no evidence that Genesis chapter 1 is not true.

Although Genesis is a narrative, one can see the poetic nature of this chapter. Most of the verses begin with, "And God called/said," and the second clause begins with "Let there be," which makes the reading of the chapter flow. This repetition also emphasizes that God alone created all things.

Verses 26–28 are significant for several reasons. This is the first time that man is mentioned and God makes a distinction with man. God states that man is made in His own image. Although it states "us" in verse 26, this does not refer to three gods. This refers to the three manifestations of God, which are God the Father,

---

[5] Some scholars believe that the days represent longer time periods than our twenty-four-hour days, which helps explain the evidence of the earth being older than the Bible seems to state.

[6] Longman, *How to Read Genesis*, 103.

[7] Erickson, *Christian Theology,* 3rd ed., 435.

[8] A theory in astronomy: the universe originated billions of years ago in a rapid expansion from a single point of nearly infinite energy density.

Jesus Christ, and the Holy Spirit. God is one God.[9] He also gives man authority over the rest of His creation. Verse 27 repeats that the male was created in God's image but now also adds that the female was also created in God's image. In verse 28, not only does God bless man and command him to multiply, but He gives man authority over all other creatures of the earth. God also states that what He created on the sixth day was very good, which makes another distinction between man and His other creations. In Genesis 1:28, He gives mankind their first command, which is to be fruitful and multiply. Only a man and a woman can produce another human, so this first commandment establishes the order God intended, which is for men and women to reproduce and have a sexual relationship. This verse does not support homosexual, bisexual, or transgender ideology. Once again, the last part of verse 28 gives humans authority and dominion over the earth. Humans have an obligation to govern according to God's laws and to use the earth's resources responsibly.

Chapter 1 establishes some characteristics of God and basic principles in reference to God's relationship with men. God created the world out of non-existence. God is one God. God created man.

Review
1. Memorize Genesis 1:1
2. Define *ex nihlo*. How is this term different from when humans create or invent things?
3. Discuss the significance of Genesis 1:26–28.
4. What do we learn about God in this first chapter?
5. Review what is created on each of the six days of creation.

---

[9] Deuteronomy 6:4

Genesis Chapter 2

1 *Thus the heavens and the earth were finished, and all the host of them.*
2 And on the seventh day God ended his work which he had made; and he rested on the seventh day from all his work which he had made.

3 And God blessed the seventh day, and sanctified it: because that in it he had rested from all his work which God created and made.

4 These are the generations of the heavens and of the earth when they were created, in the day that the LORD God made the earth and the heavens,

5 And every plant of the field before it was in the earth, and every herb of the field before it grew: for the LORD God had not caused it to rain upon the earth, and there was not a man to till the ground.

6 But there went up a mist from the earth, and watered the whole face of the ground.

7 And the LORD God formed man of the dust of the ground, and breathed into his nostrils the breath of life; and man became a living soul.

8 And the LORD God planted a garden eastward in Eden; and there he put the man whom he had formed.

9 And out of the ground made the LORD God to grow every tree that is pleasant to the sight, and good for food; the tree of life also in the midst of the garden, and the tree of knowledge of good and evil.

10 And a river went out of Eden to water the garden; and from thence it was parted, and became into four heads.

11 The name of the first is Pison: that is it which compasseth the whole land of Havilah, where there is gold;

12 And the gold of that land is good: there is bdellium and the onyx stone.

13 And the name of the second river is Gihon: the same is it that compasseth the whole land of Ethiopia.

14 And the name of the third river is Hiddekel: that is it which goeth toward the east of Assyria. And the fourth river is Euphrates.

15 And the LORD God took the man, and put him into the garden of Eden to dress it and to keep it.

16 And the LORD God commanded the man, saying, Of every tree of the garden thou mayest freely eat:

17 But of the tree of the knowledge of good and evil, thou shalt not eat of it: for in the day that thou eatest thereof thou shalt surely die.

18 And the LORD God said, It is not good that the man should be alone; I will make him an help meet for him.

19 And out of the ground the LORD God formed every beast of the field, and every fowl of the air; and brought them unto Adam to see what he would call them: and whatsoever Adam called every living creature, that was the name thereof.

20 And Adam gave names to all cattle, and to the fowl of the air, and to every beast of the field; but for Adam there was not found an help meet for him.

21 And the LORD God caused a deep sleep to fall upon Adam, and he slept: and he took one of his ribs, and closed up the flesh instead thereof;

22 And the rib, which the LORD God had taken from man, made he a woman, and brought her unto the man.

23 And Adam said, This is now bone of my bones, and flesh of my flesh: she shall be called Woman, because she was taken out of Man.

24 Therefore shall a man leave his father and his mother, and shall cleave unto his wife: and they shall be one flesh.

25 And they were both naked, the man and his wife, and were not ashamed.

Summary

vv. 1–3

God finishes creating the heavens and the earth. On the seventh day, God rests. God sanctifies and blesses the seventh day.

vv. 4–6

This is the history of the heavens and the earth. Plants flourish although there is no rain and no one to till the ground. There is a mist that comes up from the ground that provides water.

v. 7

God forms man from the dust of the earth and breathes life into him, and he becomes a living soul.

vv. 8–9

God plants a garden in Eden, and he places man there. God makes the trees and the plants flourish, and they are nice to look on, and they are good for food. The tree of the knowledge of good and evil and the tree of life are also in the garden.

vv. 10–14

A river flows out of Eden and divides into four rivers. The first one is Pison. The second is Gihon. The third is Hiddekel, and the fourth is Euphrates.

vv. 15–17

God puts Adam in the garden to take care of it. God gives Adam the commandment not to eat of the tree of good and evil. God tells Adam the consequence of eating from the tree, which is death.

vv. 18–19

God states that it is not good for Adam to be alone, and God will make Adam a suitable companion. God brings to Adam all animals and birds for Adam to name them.

vv. 20–25

There is no help mate for Adam. God causes Adam to sleep and removes a rib from him. From that rib, God forms a woman and brings her to Adam. Adam states, "This is now bone of my bones, and flesh of my flesh." A man will leave his father and mother and shall be joined to his wife, and they will be one flesh. They are both naked and not ashamed.

Commentary

God makes a distinction between the seventh day and the other days of creation. God blesses and sanctifies the seventh day. *Sanctify* means "to be set apart for God's use."[10] God sets the seventh day apart, and as Christians, we should honor God by having a day of rest and dedication to God.

---

[10] Doug Mangum, "Sanctification," in *The Lexham Bible Dictionary*, eds. John D. Barry et al. (Bellingham: Lexham Press, 2016).

The seventh day, or the sabbath day,[11] continued to be important to the Israelites throughout the Old Testament. Even today, Jewish people consider Saturday to be the sabbath and a day of rest. Today, Christians rest on the first day of the week (Sunday) because it is the day of Jesus's resurrection. Also, the number seven has a spiritual significance in that it means perfection, [12] emphasizing that God's creation is perfect.

This chapter describes more specifically how God created man. From chapter one, we already understand that man was a unique creation because only man was made in God's image and given dominion over the rest of God's creation. Here, the text describes how man is formed from the earth, and God breathes life into him, making him a living soul. Man is the only creation that has a soul.

We are also introduced to the woman in this chapter. God states that it is not good for man to be alone. This is in contrast to chapter one, where everything he made was good. God stated He was going to make a companion for Adam because as Adam is naming the birds and animals, there was a realization that Adam had no one compatible with him. The woman was uniquely created in that she was formed from an organ taken out of Adam. God presented the woman to Adam, and he recognized that she was uniquely created for him. The woman was created to offer Adam human companionship, and they were to rule together as partners. In Genesis 1:27, God refers to "them," so His blessing and His commandment to multiply and have dominion applied to them as a couple because a husband and wife are one flesh in the eyes of God.

The union between the man and the woman in this chapter represents the first marriage, and many wedding ceremonies include these verses. Marriage represents the unity of the man and the woman because they are of the same flesh. Moses states that a man is joined to his wife, not to just any woman, which emphasizes that this bond is a covenant relationship. A woman can only be called a wife if she has a husband, and a man can only be called a husband if he has a wife. Because God created marriage, regardless of how any government might define it, marriage is defined by the union of a man and a woman.

One might wonder why God would give man a tree with fruit that he cannot eat. At this point in Genesis, God does not give the reason why he creates the earth or the reason why he uniquely creates man to be different from His other creations. As Genesis progresses, Moses reveals that God desires a unique relationship of love and obedience from man. So God gives man a choice to be in a relationship with Him. The choice man has to make is to believe and trust God

---

[11] Bryan C. Babcock, "Sabbath," in *The Lexham Bible Dictionary*, eds. Barry et al.

[12] Robert D. Johnston, *Numbers in the Bible: God's Unique Design in Biblical Numbers* (Grand Rapids: Kregel Publications, 1990), 71.

so their loving relationship will continue, or to disobey God and live with the consequences. Love cannot be forced. Love must be a choice, and that is why I believe that God gave man a choice whether to eat of the tree or not.

The location of Eden is not important to understand the concept that God created a place for humans to dwell. *Eden* means "delight" and represents paradise.[13] This chapter names specific rivers and areas that many scholars believe are in present-day Iraq.[14]

Review
1. What is the significance of the seventh day?
2. What is unique about God's creation of man?
3. What instructions did God give about the tree of the knowledge of good and evil and the tree of life?
4. What is unique about God's creation of woman?
5. Describe the establishment of marriage.

---

[13] John Sailhamer, "Genesis," in *The Expositor's Bible Commentary*, 41.
[14] Ibid., 43.

Genesis Chapter 3

1 Now the serpent was more subtil than any beast of the field which the LORD God had made. And he said unto the woman, Yea, hath God said, Ye shall not eat of every tree of the garden?

2 And the woman said unto the serpent, We may eat of the fruit of the trees of the garden:

3 But of the fruit of the tree which is in the midst of the garden, God hath said, Ye shall not eat of it, neither shall ye touch it, lest ye die.

4 And the serpent said unto the woman, Ye shall not surely die:

5 For God doth know that in the day ye eat thereof, then your eyes shall be opened, and ye shall be as gods, knowing good and evil.

6 And when the woman saw that the tree was good for food, and that it was pleasant to the eyes, and a tree to be desired to make one wise, she took of the fruit thereof, and did eat, and gave also unto her husband with her; and he did eat.

7 And the eyes of them both were opened, and they knew that they were naked; and they sewed fig leaves together, and made themselves aprons.

8 And they heard the voice of the LORD God walking in the garden in the cool of the day: and Adam and his wife hid themselves from the presence of the LORD God amongst the trees of the garden.

9 And the LORD God called unto Adam, and said unto him, Where art thou?

10 And he said, I heard thy voice in the garden, and I was afraid, because I was naked; and I hid myself.

17

11 And he said, Who told thee that thou wast naked? Hast thou eaten of the tree, whereof I commanded thee that thou shouldest not eat?

12 And the man said, The woman whom thou gavest to be with me, she gave me of the tree, and I did eat.

13 And the LORD God said unto the woman, What is this that thou hast done? And the woman said, The serpent beguiled me, and I did eat.

14 And the LORD God said unto the serpent, Because thou hast done this, thou art cursed above all cattle, and above every beast of the field; upon thy belly shalt thou go, and dust shalt thou eat all the days of thy life:

15 And I will put enmity between thee and the woman, and between thy seed and her seed: it shall bruise thy head, and thou shalt bruise his heel.

16 Unto the woman he said, I will greatly multiply thy sorrow and thy conception; in sorrow thou shalt bring forth children; and thy desire shall be to thy husband, and he shall rule over thee.

17 And unto Adam he said, Because thou hast hearkened unto the voice of thy wife, and hast eaten of the tree, of which I commanded thee, saying, Thou shalt not eat of it: cursed is the ground for thy sake; in sorrow shalt thou eat of it all the days of thy life;

18 Thorns also and thistles shall it bring forth to thee; and thou shalt eat the herb of the field;

19 In the sweat of thy face shalt thou eat bread, till thou return unto the ground; for out of it wast thou taken: for dust thou art, and unto dust shalt thou return.

20 And Adam called his wife's name Eve; because she was the mother of all living.

21 Unto Adam also and to his wife did the LORD God make coats of skins, and clothed them.

22 And the LORD God said, Behold, the man is become as one of us, to know good and evil: and now, lest he put forth his hand, and take also of the tree of life, and eat, and live for ever:

23 Therefore the Lord God sent him forth from the garden of Eden, to till the ground from whence he was taken.

24 So he drove out the man; and he placed at the east of the garden of Eden Cherubims, and a flaming sword which turned every way, to keep the way of the tree of life.

Summary

v. 1

The serpent is described as more subtle than any other creature. The serpent asks the woman a question: "Hath God said, ye shall not eat of every tree in the garden?"

vv. 2–3

The woman replies that they can eat from the trees in the garden. The woman continues to say they cannot eat from the tree in the middle of the garden, or they will die.

vv. 4–5

The serpent replies that they will not die. Then the serpent continues to state that God told them this so they won't become as powerful as He is. The serpent states they will be like gods.

v. 6

When the woman examines the tree, the fruit looks good and tasty, so she eats and gives some to Adam, and he also eats.

v. 7

Adam and the woman's eyes are opened to good and evil. They realize they are naked and sew fig leaves together to make themselves clothes.

vv. 8–9

They hear God looking for them. They are ashamed and hide themselves.
God calls out to them, asking them where they are.

v. 10

Adam finally replies to God and says that he heard God but was afraid because he was naked, so he hid himself.

v. 11

God replies by asking Adam and the woman who told them that they were naked and if they ate from the tree that He told them not to eat from.

v. 12

Adam replies that the woman God gave him brought him the fruit, and he ate it.

v. 13

God asks the woman what she has done, and the woman claims that the serpent tricked her, and she ate.

vv. 14–15

God curses the serpent. He is cursed above all cattle and will be on his belly. There will also be enmity, or hatred, between the seed of the woman and the seed of the serpent. The woman's seed shall bruise the serpent's head, and the serpent's seed shall bruise His heel.

v. 16

The woman is cursed to have sorrow in conception and childbirth, and her husband will rule over her.

vv. 17–19

The man is cursed to work the land. Man was made from dust and will return to dust.

v. 20

Adam names his wife *Eve*, which means "mother of all living."

v. 21

God makes coverings out of animal skins for Adam and Eve.

vv. 22-24

God exiles Adam and Eve from the garden. He wants to prevent them from eating from the tree of life. God places cherubim and a flaming sword to guard the garden.

Commentary

This chapter describes when sin entered the world. What a fellowship we had with God! Now our flesh and Satan are constantly working against us to break up our relationship with God. How nice it must have been just to be able to talk to God without battling the flesh every day! Once sin enters the world, the Bible focuses on restoring the relationship between God and man to its original form.

The chapter begins by introducing us to Satan, represented as a serpent. This is the first time Satan is introduced in the Bible. The serpent is described as subtle. *Subtle* means "crafty, sly, and devious." Satan is *crafty*, which means "skillfully underhanded and deceptive." Satan is skillful. He just uses his skills for evil. In the first verse, the serpent begins by asking a seemingly innocent question, but his intention is to create doubt in the mind of the woman. Satan asks, "Did God really say, 'You must not eat from any tree in the garden?'" In verse 4, the serpent uses deception. He is not incorrect that they will not die, but he does not reveal the whole truth. Satan is deceptive by giving only partial truth. Although it is just a few verses from when the serpent speaks to the woman to when they eat the fruit, no one knows how long the serpent may have tried to convince her that she will not die from eating from the tree.

When God asks Adam if he ate of the tree, Adam confesses that he ate from it but implies that God is responsible because he gave the woman to Adam. The woman also blames the serpent for her actions. Although both admit to their actions, neither one takes responsibility for his or her actions. This is relevant to Christians today. Although God does forgive our sins, one must first admit one's sins and take responsibility for one's actions.

In this chapter, we can also see the significant influence a spouse has on his or her partner. Although it is recorded that the serpent only spoke to the woman, both the woman and man ate of the fruit. No one is perfect, but obviously one should choose one's spouse carefully.

Because of their actions, Adam and the woman are punished. The serpent is cursed to crawl on his belly, and there will be hatred between the seed of the serpent and seed of the woman. This is sometimes referred to as the first prophecy of Jesus Christ, in that it refers to a future conflict between their seed.[15] The woman will now have pain in childbirth, and instead of having a mutual partnership, her husband will now rule over her. The man will also have to work hard to produce food from the land. But the worst punishment of all is the change in relationship with God. Humanity will no longer have the same bond with God as before because now humanity is marred by sin.

Humanity did not die physically from eating the fruit, but the "perfect" relationship they had with God died. God also removed them from the garden of Eden so they would not have access to the tree of life. Another consequence of their disobedience was that they would return to dust and would not live forever in human flesh.

As they were being removed from the garden, Adam names the woman *Eve*. Up until this point in the text, she is always referred to as the woman or wife. Adam gives her an appropriate name because she is the mother of all living.

---

[15] Sailhamer, "Genesis," *The Expositor's Bible Commentary*, 55.

Review
1. Describe how Satan convinces Eve to disobey God.
2. Once Adam and Eve eat the fruit, their eyes are opened. Why is this significant?
3. What is the significance of Genesis 3:15?
4. What is Adam's punishment for disobedience?
5. What is Eve's punishment for disobedience?

Genesis Chapter 4

1 *And Adam knew Eve his wife; and she conceived, and bare Cain, and said, I have gotten a man from the LORD.*

2 And she again bare his brother Abel. And Abel was a keeper of sheep, but Cain was a tiller of the ground.

3 And in process of time it came to pass, that Cain brought of the fruit of the ground an offering unto the LORD.

4 And Abel, he also brought of the firstlings of his flock and of the fat thereof. And the LORD had respect unto Abel and to his offering:

5 But unto Cain and to his offering he had not respect. And Cain was very wroth, and his countenance fell.

6 And the LORD said unto Cain, Why art thou wroth? and why is thy countenance fallen?

7 If thou doest well, shalt thou not be accepted? and if thou doest not well, sin lieth at the door. And unto thee shall be his desire, and thou shalt rule over him.

8 And Cain talked with Abel his brother: and it came to pass, when they were in the field, that Cain rose up against Abel his brother, and slew him.

9 And the LORD said unto Cain, Where is Abel thy brother? And he said, I know not: Am I my brother's keeper?

10 And he said, What hast thou done? the voice of thy brother's blood crieth unto me from the ground.

11 And now art thou cursed from the earth, which hath opened her mouth to receive thy brother's blood from thy hand;

12 When thou tillest the ground, it shall not henceforth yield unto thee her strength; a fugitive and a vagabond shalt thou be in the earth.

13 And Cain said unto the LORD, My punishment is greater than I can bear.

14 Behold, thou hast driven me out this day from the face of the earth; and from thy face shall I be hid; and I shall be a fugitive and a vagabond in the earth; and it shall come to pass, that every one that findeth me shall slay me.

15 And the LORD said unto him, Therefore whosoever slayeth Cain, vengeance shall be taken on him sevenfold. And the LORD set a mark upon Cain, lest any finding him should kill him.

16 And Cain went out from the presence of the LORD, and dwelt in the land of Nod, on the east of Eden.

17 And Cain knew his wife; and she conceived, and bare Enoch: and he builded a city, and called the name of the city, after the name of his son, Enoch.

18 And unto Enoch was born Irad: and Irad begat Mehujael: and Mehujael begat Methusael: and Methusael begat Lamech.

19 And Lamech took unto him two wives: the name of the one was Adah, and the name of the other Zillah.

20 And Adah bare Jabal: he was the father of such as dwell in tents, and of such as have cattle.

21 And his brother's name was Jubal: he was the father of all such as handle the harp and organ.

22 And Zillah, she also bare Tubal-cain, an instructer of every artificer in brass and iron: and the sister of Tubal-cain was Naamah.

23 And Lamech said unto his wives, Adah and Zillah, Hear my voice; ye wives of Lamech, hearken unto my speech: for I have slain a man to my wounding, and a young man to my hurt.

24 If Cain shall be avenged sevenfold, truly Lamech seventy and sevenfold.

25 And Adam knew his wife again; and she bare a son, and called his name Seth: For God, said she, hath appointed me another seed instead of Abel, whom Cain slew.

26 And to Seth, to him also there was born a son; and he called his name Enos: then began men to call upon the name of the LORD.

Summary

vv. 1–2

Adam and Eve have two sons. The oldest is *Cain*, meaning "possession,"[16] who is a farmer, and the youngest is *Abel*, meaning "breath, vapor, transitions, short life,"[17] who is a shepherd.

vv. 3–5

Abel brings the first offering of his flock unto the Lord, and it is accepted, but Cain's offering is not accepted, and Cain becomes angry.

vv. 6–7

God asks Cain why he is upset, stating that if Cain brings an acceptable offering to the Lord, his offering will be accepted also.

v. 8

Cain kills Abel.

v. 9

The Lord asks Cain where his brother is. Cain states that he does not know and that he is not responsible for his brother.

vv. 10–12

God reveals that He knows Cain has killed his brother and places a curse on Cain for his sin.

vv. 13–15

Cain pleads that his punishment is too much. In response, God protects him by placing a mark on him and states that anyone who kills Cain will be punished sevenfold. Cain is cursed to be a wanderer.

vv. 16–24

These verses describe the generations of Cain.

vv. 25–26

---

[16] The Holy Bible, King James Version (Grand Rapids, 2010).
[17] Ibid.

Adam and Eve have another son named *Seth*, meaning "appointed."[18] Moses states that Seth is appointed to replace the seed of Abel. Also at this time, men begin to call on the name of the Lord.

Commentary

Chapter 3 details when sin enters the world. Now, this chapter presents the effect of sin, such as jealousy, revenge, murder, and exile. In the very first family, there was dysfunction. Adam's oldest son, Cain, kills his younger brother Abel. Although some people debate about why Abel's offering is accepted as opposed to Cain's offering, the important point is that Cain's offering is not acceptable to God. Because of the rejection of his offering, Cain feels such intense jealousy and hatred that he kills his own brother.

Before Cain acts on his jealousy, God asks him a rhetorical question. God states that Cain has no reason to be upset because if he does what is right, his offering will be accepted. But if not, sin will rule over him. God similarly asks Cain a question after he commits a sin, just as God asked his parents in the previous chapter. God is giving Cain a chance to admit his actions and to repent. But instead, Cain responds almost sarcastically by stating that he is not responsible for his brother.

Cain's response in verse 9 is very well-known. In popular culture, the phrase "Am I my brother's keeper?" has been used to question what our responsibility for one another is. As Christians, we are responsible for one another. We may not be responsible for another's specific choices, but we are responsible for living in such a way to promote love and not hate. As a result of his sin, Cain is cursed. The ground will no longer produce crops for him, and he is exiled to be a wanderer.

Often when a person's name is mentioned in the Bible, the meaning has significance. It may be the circumstances of his or her birth, a future prophecy, or specific characteristics of the individual. We see that this pattern begins with the first family. Adam names Eve to reflect that she is the mother of all living. Cain and Abel's names are significant in the context of their livelihoods. The chapter ends with the birth of Seth, who is appointed to carry on the righteous seed of Adam. Once Seth is born and has a son, men begin to call on the name of the Lord. This signifies that man has to acknowledge God and has to establish a relationship with God.

---

[18] The Holy Bible, King James Version (Grand Rapids, 2010).

In reference to the description of Cain's descendants, one might wonder where these people came from. The theory I most agree with is that Adam and Eve had other children but they were just not recorded.[19]

Review
1. What is the significance of the meanings of the names of Cain and Abel?
2. What was similar and what was different in God's response to Cain as compared to his parents when they sinned?
3. What is the significance of verse 9 in this text, and what is its significance today as it relates to our relationships with each other?
4. What is the significance of the meaning of Seth's name?
5. What does it mean and why is it significant that in verse 26 they begin to call on the name of the Lord?

---

[19] John H. Walton, *Genesis: The NIV Application Commentary* (Grand Rapids: Zondervan, 2001), 265.

Genesis Chapter 5

1 This is the book of the generations of Adam. In the day that God created man, in the likeness of God made he him;

2 Male and female created he them; and blessed them, and called their name Adam, in the day when they were created.

3 And Adam lived an hundred and thirty years, and begat a son in his own likeness, after his image; and called his name Seth:

4 And the days of Adam after he had begotten Seth were eight hundred years: and he begat sons and daughters:

5 And all the days that Adam lived were nine hundred and thirty years: and he died.

6 And Seth lived an hundred and five years, and begat Enos:

7 And Seth lived after he begat Enos eight hundred and seven years, and begat sons and daughters:

8 And all the days of Seth were nine hundred and twelve years: and he died.

9 And Enos lived ninety years, and begat Cainan:

10 And Enos lived after he begat Cainan eight hundred and fifteen years, and begat sons and daughters:

11 And all the days of Enos were nine hundred and five years: and he died.

12 And Cainan lived seventy years, and begat Mahalaleel:

13 And Cainan lived after he begat Mahaleel eight hundred and forty years, and begat sons and daughters:

14 And all the days of Cainan were nine hundred and ten years: and he died.

15 And Mahalaleel lived sixty and five years, and begat Jared:

16 And Mahalaleel lived after he begat Jared eight hundred and thirty years, and begat sons and daughters:

17 And all the days of Mahalaleel were eight hundred ninety and five years: and he died.

18 And Jared lived an hundred sixty and two years, and he begat Enoch:

19 And Jared lived after he begat Enoch eight hundred years, and begat sons and daughters:

20 And all the days of Jared were nine hundred sixty and two years: and he died.

21 And Enoch lived sixty and five years, and begat Methuselah:

22 And Enoch walked with God after he begat Methuselah three hundred years, and begat sons and daughters:

23 And all the days of Enoch were three hundred sixty and five years:

24 And Enoch walked with God: and he was not; for God took him.

25 And Methuselah lived an hundred eighty and seven years, and begat Lamech:

26 And Methuselah lived after he begat Lamech seven hundred eighty and two years, and begat sons and daughters:

27 And all the days of Methuselah were nine hundred sixty and nine years: and he died.

28 And Lamech lived an hundred eighty and two years, and begat a son:

29 And he called his name Noah, saying, this same shall comfort us concerning our work and toil of our hands, because of the ground which the LORD hath cursed.

30 And Lamech lived after he begat Noah five hundred ninety and five years, and begat sons and daughters:

31 And all the days of Lamech were seven hundred seventy and seven years: and he died.

32 And Noah was five hundred years old: and Noah begat Shem, Ham, and Japheth.

Summary

vv. 1–32

These verses summarize the generations from Adam's son Seth to Noah.

Commentary

This chapter records the lineage of Adam to Noah. In verse 2, it is noted that God named "them" Adam. This expresses that a husband and wife are one in God's eyes. Eve is the name Adam gave his wife.

This chapter also gives us an example of a righteous man in Enoch. Enoch is noteworthy because he walked with God and did not die. He is an example of a man who was righteous before God and did not suffer the consequence of sin, which is death.

Methuselah is also worthy of note because he lived the longest time. He died at 969 years. It is from his long life that we have the expression "as old as Methuselah," expressing someone being extremely old.

Noah means "He will comfort us."[20] The significance of his name is reflected in the next several chapters as Noah is chosen to save humanity.

Review
1. Discuss the meaning and application of verse 2.
2. Why is Enoch significant?
3. Why is Methuselah significant?
4. What is the significance of Noah's name?

---

[20] Sailhamer, "Genesis," in *The Expositor's Bible Commentary*, 74.

Genesis Chapter 6

1 *And it came to pass, when men began to multiply on the face of the earth, and daughters were born unto them,*

2 That the sons of God saw the daughters of men that they were fair; and they took them wives of all which they chose.

3 And the LORD said, My spirit shall not always strive with man, for that he also is flesh: yet his days shall be an hundred and twenty years.

4 There were giants in the earth in those days; and also after that, when the sons of God came in unto the daughters of men, and they bare children to them, the same became mighty men which were of old, men of renown.

5 And God saw that the wickedness of man was great in the earth, and that every imagination of the thoughts of his heart was only evil continually.

6 And it repented the LORD that he had made man on the earth, and it grieved him at his heart.

7 And the LORD said, I will destroy man whom I have created from the face of the earth; both man, and beast, and the creeping thing, and the fowls of the air; for it repenteth me that I have made them.

8 But Noah found grace in the eyes of the LORD.

9 These are the generations of Noah: Noah was a just man and perfect in his generations, and Noah walked with God.

10 And Noah begat three sons, Shem, Ham, and Japheth.

11 The earth also was corrupt before God, and the earth was filled with violence.

12 And God looked upon the earth, and, behold, it was corrupt; for all flesh had corrupted his way upon the earth.

13 And God said unto Noah, The end of all flesh is come before me; for the earth is filled with violence through them; and, behold, I will destroy them with the earth.

14 Make thee an ark of gopher wood; rooms shalt thou make in the ark, and shalt pitch it within and without with pitch.

15 And this is the fashion which thou shalt make it of: The length of the ark shall be three hundred cubits, the breadth of it fifty cubits, and the height of it thirty cubits.

16 A window shalt thou make to the ark, and in a cubit shalt thou finish it above; and the door of the ark shalt thou set in the side thereof: with lower, second, and third stories shalt thou make it.

17 And, behold, I, even I, do bring a flood of waters upon the earth, to destroy all flesh, wherein is the breath of life, from under heaven; and every thing that is in the earth shall die.

18 But with thee will I establish my covenant; and thou shalt come into the ark, thou, and thy sons, and thy wife, and thy sons' wives with thee.

19 And of every living thing of all flesh, two of every sort shalt thou bring into the ark, to keep them alive with thee; they shall be male and female.

20 Of fowls after their kind, and of cattle after their kind, of every creeping thing of the earth after his kind, two of every sort shall come unto thee, to keep them alive.

21 And take thou unto thee of all food that is eaten, and thou shalt gather it to thee; and it shall be for food for thee, and for them.

22 Thus did Noah; according to all that God commanded him, so did he.

Summary

vv. 1–3

People begin to multiply on the earth. The sons of God see the daughters of men and take them for their wives. God states His spirit will not be with man for a long time, and man's days will be 120 years.

vv. 4–7

There are giants on the earth. When they reproduce with the daughters of men, they have children who are mighty men and famous. God sees that man has become wicked and his thoughts are always evil. God is sorry that he has made man and decides he will destroy man, cattle, birds, and every living thing.

vv. 8–10

Noah finds grace in the eyes of the Lord. Noah is just and upright and walks with God. Noah has three sons: Shem, Ham, and Japheth.

vv. 11–13

The earth is corrupt and filled with violence. God tells Noah that he is going to destroy the earth because of the corruption and violence.

vv. 14–16

God gives Noah instructions on how to build the ark. The ark is to be made out of gopher wood (cypress wood).[21] The ark will have rooms and will have pitch[22] (or be waterproofed with tar) inside it and outside it. It will be 300 cubits[23] in length. It will be 50 cubits[24] in width and 30 cubits[25] in height. There will be a window for light measuring one cubit, and it will have three stories and one door.

vv. 17–22

God states there will be a flood to destroy all life, but He will establish a covenant with Noah and his family, and they will go into the ark. God gives Noah instructions on what animals and food to bring. Noah does what God instructs him to do.

Commentary

There are several interesting items in this chapter. Who are the sons of God? Who are the giants? Who are the mighty men? What does it mean when God says His spirit will not always strive with men and that man's days will be 120 years? Why does it state that God repented?

There are three main views that have been used to explain "the sons of God." The first one is that it refers to Seth's descendants. The second is that it refers to angels, and the third is that it refers to kings, rulers, or noblemen. The term "giants" here is defined as "Nephilim," which has been used to mean "men of great size" or "men of a great name."[26] The combination of the sons of God and the daughters of men produces mighty men or men who are great warriors.

---

[21] Gordon J. Wenham, *Word Biblical Commentary*, vol. 1, *Genesis 1-15* (Grand Rapids: Zondervan, 1987), 172.

[22] Wenham, *Word Biblical Commentary*, 1:173.

[23] Walton, *Genesis*. 312.
1 cubit = 18 inches. 300 cubits is 450 feet or 137 meters.

[24] 50 cubits = 75 feet

[25] 30 cubits = 45 feet

[26] Walton, Genesis, 77.

Regardless of which view one chooses, Moses is stating that mankind has married, multiplied, and is in a sinful state. He describes the depths of man's sin in verse 5: "every imagination of the thoughts of his heart was only evil continually." Because of the extent of mankind's sin, God decides to destroy man and all living creatures.

In my opinion, there are two views of Genesis 6:3 in reference to man's lifespan being 120 years. One view is that God has determined that every man's lifespan will be 120 years, just as it is stated in the text. This view is contradicted in that many people continue to live much longer than that after this statement is made. The second view is that God warns Noah about the flood 120 years before it occurs.[27]

Does God repent? According to Numbers 23:19, God does not repent. The Hebrew word *wayyinnāhem* used in Genesis 6:6 means "sorry." God regrets that man has chosen to do evil and that he has to punish them with the consequences of their choices. Because of the limitation of human speech, "repent" is used as the best way to express God's emotions in this situation.

Although mankind has become evil, Noah stands out in contrast to all other mankind. Moses describes Noah as just and perfect. He also walks with God. This is the same expression used with Enoch. God makes a covenant with Noah. This is the first time the word *covenant* is used in the Bible. *Covenant* denotes "a gracious undertaking entered into by God for the benefit and blessing of humanity, and specifically of those who by faith receive the promises and commit themselves to the obligations which this undertaking involves."[28] God establishes that he will keep Noah and his family safe and alive. This is characteristic of the Old Testament covenants. God chooses a man who is righteous and faithful and promises him supernatural blessings. I use the term *supernatural* because in each covenant, whether it is Abrahamic, Mosaic, or Davidic, the blessings that God bestows can only be done by God and cannot be accomplished by human means.

The King James Version of the Bible uses "ark" to describe the vessel that Noah built. We commonly do not use the term "ark" when describing a seafaring vessel. Other verses in the Bible use the term "boat" or "ship" when describing vessels on the water. One of Merriam-Webster's definitions of *ark* is "something that affords safety." I believe Moses uses this term to emphasize that it was a vessel to keep Noah and his family safe.[29]

---

[27] Sailhamer, "Genesis," in *The Expositor's Bible Commentary*, 76–77.

[28] G. L. Archer Jr., "Covenant," in *Evangelical Dictionary of Theology*, 2nd ed., ed. Walter Elwell (Grand Rapids: Baker Book House, 2001), 299.

[29] It is also used in Exodus 2:3 to describe the basket that Moses's mother placed him in to keep him safe.

Interesting Noah Facts
1. The ark was the largest seagoing vessel known before the twentieth century.[30]
2. Noah and his family were in the ark for fifty-three weeks.
3. The total floor space inside the ark was 100,000 square feet.[31]
4. The ark's cubic volume was 1,518,000 cubic feet.[32]
5. There was no such thing as rain before the flood.

Review
1. What explanation do you think best describes the "sons of God," "daughters of men," "giants," and "mighty men," which are listed in verses 1–4?
2. What does verse 3 mean when it states, "his days shall be a hundred and twenty years?"
3. Is verse 5 still an accurate description of humanity today? If yes, then describe in what ways and give some examples. If no, then state why not.
4. In verse 6, it states that God repented. What is meant by this term in reference to God?
5. What does the text mean in verse 9 when it states that Noah walked with God? Which other person in the Bible "walked with God"?

---

[30] Francis A. Schaeffer, *Genesis in Space and Time* (Downers Grove: InterVarsity Press, 1972), 130.

[31] Ibid., 130.

[32] Schaeffer, *Genesis in Space and Time*, 130.

Genesis Chapter 7

1 And the LORD said unto Noah, Come thou and all thy house into the ark; for thee have I seen righteous before me in this generation.

2 Of every clean beast thou shalt take to thee by sevens, the male and his female: and of beasts that are not clean by two, the male and his female.

3 Of fowls also of the air by sevens, the male and the female; to keep seed alive upon the face of all the earth.

4 For yet seven days, and I will cause it to rain upon the earth forty days and forty nights; and every living substance that I have made will I destroy from off the face of the earth.

5 And Noah did according unto all that the LORD commanded him.

6 And Noah was six hundred years old when the flood of waters was upon the earth.

7 And Noah went in, and his sons, and his wife, and his sons' wives with him, into the ark, because of the waters of the flood.

8 Of clean beasts, and of beasts that are not clean, and of fowls, and of every thing that creepeth upon the earth,

9 There went in two and two unto Noah into the ark, the male and the female, as God had commanded Noah.

10 And it came to pass after seven days, that the waters of the flood were upon the earth.

11 In the six hundredth year of Noah's life, in the second month, the seventeenth day of the month, the same day were all the fountains of the great deep broken up, and the windows of heaven were opened.

12 And the rain was upon the earth forty days and forty nights.

13 In the selfsame day entered Noah, and Shem, and Ham, and Japheth, the sons of Noah, and Noah's wife, and the three wives of his sons with them, into the ark;

14 They, and every beast after his kind, and all the cattle after their kind, and every creeping thing that creepeth upon the earth after his kind, and every fowl after his kind, every bird of every sort.

15 And they went in unto Noah into the ark, two and two of all flesh, wherein is the breath of life.

16 And they that went in, went in male and female of all flesh, as God had commanded him: and the LORD shut him in.

17 And the flood was forty days upon the earth; and the waters increased, and bare up the ark, and it was lift up above the earth.

18 And the waters prevailed, and were increased greatly upon the earth; and the ark went upon the face of the waters.

19 And the waters prevailed exceedingly upon the earth; and all the high hills, that were under the whole heaven, were covered.

20 Fifteen cubits upward did the waters prevail; and the mountains were covered.

21 And all flesh died that moved upon the earth, both of fowl, and of cattle, and of beast, and of every creeping thing that creepeth upon the earth, and every man:

22 All in whose nostrils was the breath of life, of all that was in the dry land, died.

23 And every living substance was destroyed which was upon the face of the ground, both man, and cattle, and the creeping things, and the fowl of the heaven; and they were destroyed from the earth: and Noah only remained alive, and they that were with him in the ark.

24 And the waters prevailed upon the earth an hundred and fifty days.

Summary

vv. 1–4

God informs Noah that he and his family will go into the ark because God has seen that Noah has been righteous in his generation. Noah should take one pair of unclean animals and seven pairs of clean animals. He should also bring seven pairs of birds to keep their species alive. In seven days, God states that it will rain for forty days and forty nights, and every living thing on the earth will be destroyed.

vv. 5–10

Noah follows God's instructions. Noah is six hundred years old when the flood starts. He and his family and the animals that God identifies all board the ark, and after seven days the flood starts.

vv. 11–17

When Noah is six hundred years old, in the second month on the seventeenth day, the flood begins. The rain lasts for forty days. Moses states that Noah, his wife, his sons, and their wives are all on the ark. Every animal, bird, and any other living thing in pairs of male and female are also on the ark. The water increases for forty days and lifts the ark above the earth.

vv. 18–24

The water covers the earth up to 15 cubits,[33] and it covers the mountains. Every human and every living creature on dry land dies. Only Noah and his family live. The waters are on the earth for 150 days.

Commentary

Throughout the Bible, numbers have significance. This chapter starts with God telling Noah that the rain will start in seven days and that he should bring seven clean animals. The biblical significance of the number seven is that of spiritual perfection.[34] There will be spiritual perfection in seven days because the sinful will die and the righteous will be saved. Noah is also instructed to bring seven clean animals, which will be used for food and for sacrifice after they leave the ark.

Although there is no description of clean or unclean animals at this point in the Bible, the Israelites who were the original audience understood the difference between clean and unclean animals.[35] The dietary and animal sacrifice guidelines were given to establish the Israelites as God's chosen people. As God's chosen people, the Israelites had to fulfill these requirements to be holy and to maintain their relationship with God. Even this early in the plan for redemption, God was establishing guidelines for holiness.

---

[33] 15 cubits = 22.5 feet
[34] Johnston, *Numbers in the Bible*, 71.
[35] Leviticus 11

The number forty is also repeated five times in this chapter to describe the length of time that it will rain. The biblical significance of the number forty is *trial*. It is the period of full probation or of complete testing.[36] The forty days of rain is a time of testing for Noah and his family. Noah and his family pass this trial by being obedient to God's instructions and are able to reap the benefits of God's blessings.

Genesis 2:7 states that God "breathed into the nostrils the breath of life." In this chapter in verse 15, those in the ark have the breath of life, and those outside the ark lose their breath of life. The very life that God gave them is taken away because of their disobedience.

In the New Testament, baptism is established as a symbol of washing away one's sins and beginning a new covenant relationship with Jesus. The flood symbolizes a type of baptism. The water destroys all those who are sinful and establishes a new covenant with Noah and his family who are righteous. Noah is also considered to be an Old Testament type of Jesus Christ.[37] Noah is righteous, and because of his righteousness, humanity is saved. Now that God has established a covenant with Noah, he repeats many of the same commands as in the first chapter of Genesis. Noah might be considered a second "Adam" because he is the father of the only surviving family, and it is through his descendants that the earth is repopulated.

Review
1. What is the biblical significance of the number seven?
2. What is the biblical significance of the number forty?
3. What is significant about "the breath of life" in verse 22 in reference to Genesis 2:7?
4. How is the flood symbolic of the New Testament Christian baptism?
5. Discuss how Noah is a type of Christ and can be considered the new Adam.

---

[36] Johnston, *Numbers in the Bible*, 85.

[37] Typology is a literary hermeneutical device in which a person, event, or institution in the Old Testament is understood to correspond with a person, event, or institution in the New Testament.
Daniel J. Cameron, "Typology," in *The Lexham Bible Dictionary*, eds. John D. Barry et al.

Genesis Chapter 8

1 *And God remembered Noah, and every living thing, and all the cattle that was with him in the ark: and God made a wind to pass over the earth, and the waters assuaged;*

2 The fountains also of the deep and the windows of heaven were stopped, and the rain from heaven was restrained;

3 And the waters returned from off the earth continually: and after the end of the hundred and fifty days the waters were abated.

4 And the ark rested in the seventh month, on the seventeenth day of the month, upon the mountains of Ararat.

5 And the waters decreased continually until the tenth month: in the tenth month, on the first day of the month, were the tops of the mountains seen.

6 And it came to pass at the end of forty days, that Noah opened the window of the ark which he had made:

7 And he sent forth a raven, which went forth to and fro, until the waters were dried up from off the earth.

8 Also he sent forth a dove from him, to see if the waters were abated from off the face of the ground;

9 But the dove found no rest for the sole of her foot, and she returned unto him into the ark, for the waters were on the face of the whole earth: then he put forth his hand, and took her, and pulled her in unto him

10 And he stayed yet other seven days; and again he sent forth the dove out of the ark;

11 And the dove came in to him in the evening; and, lo, in her mouth was an olive leaf pluckt off: so Noah knew that the waters were abated from off the earth.

12 And he stayed yet other seven days; and sent forth the dove; which returned not again unto him any more.

13 And it came to pass in the six hundredth and first year, in the first month, the first day of the month, the waters were dried up from off the earth: and Noah removed the covering of the ark, and looked, and, behold, the face of the ground was dry.

14 And in the second month, on the seven and twentieth day of the month, was the earth dried.

15 And God spake unto Noah, saying,

16 Go forth of the ark, thou, and thy wife, and thy sons, and thy sons' wives with thee.

17 Bring forth with thee every living thing that is with thee, of all flesh, both of fowl, and of cattle, and of every creeping thing that creepeth upon the earth; that they may breed abundantly in the earth, and be fruitful, and multiply upon the earth.

18 And Noah went forth, and his sons, and his wife, and his sons' wives with him:

19 Every beast, every creeping thing, and every fowl, and whatsoever creepeth upon the earth, after their kinds, went forth out of the ark.

20 And Noah builded an altar unto the LORD; and took of every clean beast, and of every clean fowl, and offered burnt offerings on the altar.

21 And the LORD smelled a sweet savour; and the LORD said in his heart, I will not again curse the ground any more for man's sake; for the imagination of man's heart is evil from his youth; neither will I again smite any more every thing living, as I have done.

22 While the earth remaineth, seedtime and harvest, and cold and heat, and summer and winter, and day and night shall not cease.

Summary

vv. 1–5

God remembers Noah and those in the ark and sends a wind to dry up the earth. The waters continue to recede from the earth. After 150 days, on the seventh month on the seventeenth day, the ark stops on the mountains of Ararat. The waters continue to recede until the tenth month on the first day of the month.

vv. 6–12

After forty days, Noah sends out a raven, and it flies throughout the earth until the water dries up. He then sends out a dove, and it comes back because it can find no place to rest the soles of her feet. Noah waits another seven days and sends out a dove again, and it brings back an olive leaf. Noah waits another seven days and sends out the dove, and it does not come back.

v. 13

Noah is 601 years old in the first month on the first day when Noah removes the covering of the ark, and the ground is dry.

vv. 14–19

In the second month on the twenty-seventh day, the earth is dry, and God tells Noah that he and his family and all the animals and birds can leave the ark.

vv. 20–22

Noah builds an altar and sacrifices the clean animals to the Lord. The Lord is pleased with Noah's offering. Although man's desires are evil from his youth, God will not curse the ground because of man again. There will always be planting and harvest, hot and cold, summer and winter, and day and night.

Commentary

This chapter describes the water receding and Noah and his family being able to leave the ark. God remembers Noah and proceeds to remove the water from the earth. Noah first sends out a raven and then a dove to determine the level of the water. The second time Noah sends out the dove, she brings back an olive branch. Even today, the dove and olive branch are considered to be symbols of peace.[38]

Even after Noah knows the waters are gone, he still waits for instruction from the Lord. Noah is 600 years old in the second month on the seventeenth day when the flood starts, and when he is 601 years old in the second month on the twenty-seventh day, God tells Noah he can leave the ark. Noah's family is in the ark for approximately one year and ten days.

When God instructs Noah and his family to leave the ark, he repeats His commandment from Genesis 1:24–25 for the animals to be fruitful and multiply. Once Noah leaves the ark, the first thing he does is to build an altar and offer a sacrifice to God. God is pleased with Noah's sacrifice and states that he will not curse the ground because of men again. Despite God's punishment of death for the unrighteous, we can still see God's grace and compassion. Although the flood is over, God acknowledges that the intent of humans' hearts is still geared toward

---

[38] Schaeffer, *Genesis in Space and Time*, 144.

evil, but as long as the earth remains, he will not destroy all living creatures in this way again. This is a new beginning for God's creation.

Review
1. What does verse 1 mean when it states that God "remembered" Noah?
2. What is the significance of the dove and the olive branch to Noah and to us today?
3. How is verse 17 similar to Genesis 1:24-25, and why is this significant?
4. Why do you think Noah offers a sacrifice after he leaves the ark?
5. Discuss the significance of verses 21–22.

Genesis Chapter 9

1   *And God blessed Noah and his sons, and said unto them, Be fruitful, and multiply, and replenish the earth.*

2 And the fear of you and the dread of you shall be upon every beast of the earth, and upon every fowl of the air, upon all that moveth upon the earth, and upon all the fishes of the sea; into your hand are they delivered.

3 Every moving thing that liveth shall be meat for you; even as the green herb have I given you all things.

4 But flesh with the life thereof, which is the blood thereof, shall ye not eat.

5 And surely your blood of your lives will I require; at the hand of every beast will I require it, and at the hand of man; at the hand of every man's brother will I require the life of man.

6 Whoso sheddeth man's blood, by man shall his blood be shed: for in the image of God made he man.

7 And you, be ye fruitful, and multiply; bring forth abundantly in the earth, and multiply therein.

8 And God spake unto Noah, and to his sons with him, saying,

9 And I, behold, I establish my covenant with you, and with your seed after you;

10 And with every living creature that is with you, of the fowl, of the cattle, and of every beast of the earth with you; from all that go out of the ark, to every beast of the earth.

11 And I will establish my covenant with you; neither shall all flesh be cut off any more by the waters of a flood; neither shall there any more be a flood to destroy the earth.

12 And God said, This is the token of the covenant which I make between me and you and every living creature that is with you, for perpetual generations:

13 I do set my bow in the cloud, and it shall be for a token of a covenant between me and the earth.

14 And it shall come to pass, when I bring a cloud over the earth, that the bow shall be seen in the cloud:

15 And I will remember my covenant, which is between me and you and every living creature of all flesh; and the waters shall no more become a flood to destroy all flesh.

16 And the bow shall be in the cloud; and I will look upon it, that I may remember the everlasting covenant between God and every living creature of all flesh that is upon the earth.

17 And God said unto Noah, This is the token of the covenant, which I have established between me and all flesh that is upon the earth.

18 And the sons of Noah, that went forth of the ark, were Shem, and Ham, and Japheth: and Ham is the father of Canaan.

19 These are the three sons of Noah: and of them was the whole earth overspread.

20 And Noah began to be an husbandman, and he planted a vineyard:

21 And he drank of the wine, and was drunken; and he was uncovered within his tent.

22 And Ham, the father of Canaan, saw the nakedness of his father, and told his two brethren without.

23 And Shem and Japheth took a garment, and laid it upon both their shoulders, and went backward, and covered the nakedness of their father; and their faces were backward, and they saw not their father's nakedness.

24 And Noah awoke from his wine, and knew what his younger son had done unto him.

25 And he said, Cursed be Canaan; a servant of servants shall he be unto his brethren.

26 And he said, Blessed be the LORD God of Shem; and Canaan shall be his servant.

27 God shall enlarge Japheth, and he shall dwell in the tents of Shem; and Canaan shall be his servant.

28 And Noah lived after the flood three hundred and fifty years.

29 And all the days of Noah were nine hundred and fifty years: and he died.

Summary

v. 1

God blesses Noah and his sons and tells them to be fruitful and multiply.

vv. 2–4

Now animals and birds will fear humans because humans will be able to kill them for food instead of just eating vegetables. But humans are prohibited from eating animals with their lifeblood in them.

vv. 5–6

When a person or an animal kills a human, that person or animal must be put to death because a life is required for the life taken since man is made in the image of God.

v. 7

God tells Noah and his family to be fruitful and multiply on the earth.

vv. 8–17

God establishes his covenant with Noah, his descendants, and all living creatures that he will not destroy the earth by flood and that the rainbow will be the sign of this covenant.

vv. 18–19

The sons of Noah are Shem, Ham, and Japheth, and Ham is the father of Canaan. Noah's sons' descendants repopulate the earth.

vv. 20–27

Noah plants a vineyard. Noah becomes drunk and lies uncovered in his tent. Ham, who is the father of Canaan, discovers Noah's nakedness and tells his brothers. Shem and Japheth cover Noah instead of looking on his nakedness. When Noah wakes up and realizes what Ham has done, he curses Canaan and states he will be a servant to his brothers. Noah blesses Shem and he says God will bless Japheth with increased land, and he will dwell in the tents of Shem, and Canaan will be his servant.

vv. 28–29

Noah lives 350 years after the flood, and he dies at 950 years.

Commentary

The flood is over, and this is a new start for humanity. God establishes a covenant with Noah that is still active today. God gives the sign of the rainbow as a reminder of the covenant he has made with Noah that God will not destroy the earth with water again. God repeats and emphasizes that Noah's sons should be fruitful and multiply and commands them to repopulate the earth.

There is much debate about why Ham exposing Noah's nakedness is such a terrible act. Regardless of the reason, the point is that Ham acts unrighteously in contrast to Shem and Japheth who act righteously. Because of Ham's actions, his son Canaan is cursed. This also points out the complexities of the characters in Genesis. Although Noah is a righteous man and God decides to save him from the flood, he is not a perfect man without sin because it is his sinful choice that exposes his nakedness.

The author makes a point of stating that Ham is the father of Canaan. This was significant to the original audience of the Israelites because the Canaanites were an enemy to them at that time. Although Ham commits the sin, it is his descendants through Canaan who are cursed.

Main Points of the Flood Story
1. Humanity had become consistently evil.
2. Only Noah is righteous.
3. God decides to make a new start with Noah and his family.
4. The flood represents the first baptism by wiping away the old and starting new.
5. Noah and his family are to replenish the earth.
6. Noah starts by building an altar and making a sacrifice.
7. There is a covenant that God gives Noah, and the sign is a rainbow.
8. God will not destroy the earth with a flood again.
9. Noah is a type of Christ in that he saves those who are righteous and is also the second Adam because he restarts the human race.

Review
1. Discuss the similarities between verse 1 and Genesis 1:28.
2. What are the similarities between verse 6 and Genesis 1:27?
3. What covenant does God make with Noah? What are man's obligations, and what are God's obligations? What sign does God make in remembrance of this covenant?
4. Why does Noah curse Canaan?
5. Why is Noah considered a type of Christ?

Genesis Chapter 10

1 *Now these are the generations of the sons of Noah, Shem, Ham, and Japheth: and unto them were sons born after the flood.*

2 The sons of Japheth; Gomer, and Magog, and Madai, and Javan, and Tubal, and Meshech, and Tiras.

3 And the sons of Gomer; Ashkenaz, and Riphath, and Togarmah.

4 And the sons of Javan; Elishah, and Tarshish, Kittim, and Dodanim.

5 By these were the isles of the Gentiles divided in their lands; every one after his tongue, after their families, in their nations.

6 And the sons of Ham; Cush, and Mizraim, and Phut, and Canaan.

7 And the sons of Cush; Seba, and Havilah, and Sabtah, and Raamah, and Sabtecha: and the sons of Raamah; Sheba, and Dedan.

8 And Cush begat Nimrod: he began to be a mighty one in the earth.

9 He was a mighty hunter before the LORD: wherefore it is said, Even as Nimrod the mighty hunter before the LORD.

10 And the beginning of his kingdom was Babel, and Erech, and Accad, and Calneh, in the land of Shinar.

11 Out of that land went forth Asshur, and builded Nineveh, and the city Rehoboth, and Calah,

12 And Resen between Nineveh and Calah: the same is a great city.

13 And Mizraim begat Ludim, and Anamim, and Lehabim, and Naphtuhim,

14 And Pathrusim, and Casluhim, (out of whom came Philistim,) and Caphtorim.

15 And Canaan begat Sidon his firstborn, and Heth,

16 And the Jebusite, and the Amorite, and the Girgasite,

17 And the Hivite, and the Arkite, and the Sinite,

18 And the Arvadite, and the Zemarite, and the Hamathite: and afterward were the families of the Canaanites spread abroad.

19 And the border of the Canaanites was from Sidon, as thou comest to Gerar, unto Gaza; as thou goest, unto Sodom, and Gomorrah, and Admah, and Zeboim, even unto Lasha.

20 These are the sons of Ham, after their families, after their tongues, in their countries, and in their nations.

21 Unto Shem also, the father of all the children of Eber, the brother of Japheth the elder, even to him were children born.

22 The children of Shem; Elam, and Asshur, and Arphaxad, and Lud, and Aram.

23 And the children of Aram; Uz, and Hul, and Gether, and Mash.

24 And Arphaxad begat Salah; and Salah begat Eber.

25 And unto Eber were born two sons: the name of one was Peleg; for in his days was the earth divided; and his brother's name was Joktan.

26 And Joktan begat Almodad, and Sheleph, and Hazarmaveth, and Jerah,

27 And Hadoram, and Uzal, and Diklah,

28 And Obal, and Abimael, and Sheba,

29 And Ophir, and Havilah, and Jobab: all these were the sons of Joktan.

30 And their dwelling was from Mesha, as thou goest unto Sephar a mount of the east.

31 These are the sons of Shem, after their families, after their tongues, in their lands, after their nations.

32 These are the families of the sons of Noah, after their generations, in their nations: and by these were the nations divided in the earth after the flood.

Summary and Commentary

This is the genealogy of Noah and his sons. Obviously, this is not a complete list of every person in the world, but the author points out those who are significant to the Israelites.[39] This is not a significant chapter in understanding the purpose of Genesis, but it does help in understanding how Noah's three sons begin to repopulate the earth.

The author does give special attention to Nimrod and to Canaan. Nimrod is noted to be a mighty man and a mighty hunter, and he founds the city of Babylon, which is discussed further in chapter 11. The author also takes time to describe

---

[39] Walton, Genesis, 369.

the boundaries of the Canaanites because at the time this would have been significant to the Israelites. The land that God eventually promises to Abraham and his descendants is the land of Canaan.

Review
1. What is the significance of this chapter?
2. Why is Nimrod significant?
3. Why is Babel significant?
4. Why is it important to the Israelites to describe the border of Canaan?
5. What is the significance of Sodom and Gomorrah?

Genesis Chapter 11

1   *And the whole earth was of one language, and of one speech.*
2 And it came to pass, as they journeyed from the east, that they found a plain in the land of Shinar; and they dwelt there.

3 And they said one to another, Go to, let us make brick, and burn them throughly. And they had brick for stone, and slime had they for morter.

4 And they said, Go to, let us build us a city and a tower, whose top may reach unto heaven; and let us make us a name, lest we be scattered abroad upon the face of the whole earth.

5 And the LORD came down to see the city and the tower, which the children of men builded.

6 And the LORD said, Behold, the people is one, and they have all one language; and this they begin to do: and now nothing will be restrained from them, which they have imagined to do.

7 Go to, let us go down, and there confound their language, that they may not understand one another's speech.

8 So the LORD scattered them abroad from thence upon the face of all the earth: and they left off to build the city.

9 Therefore is the name of it called Babel; because the LORD did there confound the language of all the earth: and from thence did the LORD scatter them abroad upon the face of all the earth.

10 These are the generations of Shem: Shem was an hundred years old, and begat Arphaxad two years after the flood:

11 And Shem lived after he begat Arphaxad five hundred years, and begat sons and daughters.

12 And Arphaxad lived five and thirty years, and begat Salah:

13 And Arphaxad lived after he begat Salah four hundred and three years, and begat sons and daughters.

14 And Salah lived thirty years, and begat Eber:

15 And Salah lived after he begat Eber four hundred and three years, and begat sons and daughters.

16 And Eber lived four and thirty years, and begat Peleg:

17 And Eber lived after he begat Peleg four hundred and thirty years, and begat sons and daughters.

18 And Peleg lived thirty years, and begat Reu:

19 And Peleg lived after he begat Reu two hundred and nine years, and begat sons and daughters.

20 And Reu lived two and thirty years, and begat Serug:

21 And Reu lived after he begat Serug two hundred and seven years, and begat sons and daughters.

22 And Serug lived thirty years, and begat Nahor:

23 And Serug lived after he begat Nahor two hundred years, and begat sons and daughters.

24 And Nahor lived nine and twenty years, and begat Terah:

25 And Nahor lived after he begat Terah an hundred and nineteen years, and begat sons and daughters.

26 And Terah lived seventy years, and begat Abram, Nahor, and Haran.

27 Now these are the generations of Terah: Terah begat Abram, Nahor, and Haran; and Haran begat Lot.

28 And Haran died before his father Terah in the land of his nativity, in Ur of the Chaldees.

29 And Abram and Nahor took them wives: the name of Abram's wife was Sarai; and the name of Nahor's wife, Milcah, the daughter of Haran, the father of Milcah, and the father of Iscah.

30 But Sarai was barren; she had no child.

31 And Terah took Abram his son, and Lot the son of Haran his son's son, and Sarai his daughter in law, his son Abram's wife; and they went forth with them from Ur of the Chaldees, to go into the land of Canaan; and they came unto Haran, and dwelt there.

32 And the days of Terah were two hundred and five years: and Terah died in Haran.

Summary

vv. 1–4

There is only one language. The people come to an area called Shinar and decide to stay there. They have the ability to make bricks and decide to build a city and a tower that will reach heaven. They want to make a name for themselves, and they do not want to be scattered across the earth.

vv. 5–9

The Lord comes to see what the people are doing. God decides to introduce several languages to confuse the people because, as a unified group, they can accomplish what they have set out to do. As a result of the several languages, the Lord scatters the people across the earth. The city is named *Babel*, which means "confusion."[40]

vv. 10–32

This is the genealogy of the descendants of Shem.

Commentary

This is a transitional chapter. The first eleven chapters of Genesis describe God's relationship with all of humanity. From chapter 12 until the end of Genesis, Moses details the life of a chosen man and his descendants and their relationship with God.

Although teachers and preachers may use this passage to emphasize the strength of unity or the downfall of pride, this passage is significant because it describes how humanity spread throughout the earth and how different languages developed.

God confounds the languages because He knows the people will be able to do whatever they decide to do. As discussed earlier, humanity's imaginations or thoughts are geared toward evil.[41] So God stops their "evil" plan.

There are two possible offenses that the people make. One is pride, by desiring to make a name for themselves or to make themselves great. The other is disobedience because God commands them to scatter and fill the earth, but they do not.

This chapter ends with another list of descendants. There are several significant points in this genealogy that help the reader better understand the rest of Genesis. This genealogy shows the link between Noah and Abram and gives background information for the story of Abram. Sarai, Abram's wife, is described

---

[40] Schaeffer, *Genesis in Space and Time*, 153.
[41] Genesis 8:21

as barren. This is the first time anyone is mentioned as barren in Genesis, and this fact is very significant to the story of Abram and to the Israelites. Moses also informs the reader that Abram's family has left Ur and is on their way to Canaan but stops in Haran. The reader can also see that the lifespans are becoming shorter.

Review
1. Why do the people want to build a tower?
2. Discuss the meaning of verse 6.
3. What does Babel mean, and how is the meaning applicable to this chapter?
4. What is significant about the genealogy at the end of this chapter in relation to the rest of Genesis?
5. Discuss the importance of verse 30 and why it is important to the Israelites.

Genesis Chapter 12

1 Now the LORD had said unto Abram, Get thee out of thy country, and from thy kindred, and from thy father's house, unto a land that I will shew thee:

2 And I will make of thee a great nation, and I will bless thee, and make thy name great; and thou shalt be a blessing:

3 And I will bless them that bless thee, and curse him that curseth thee: and in thee shall all families of the earth be blessed.

4 So Abram departed, as the LORD had spoken unto him; and Lot went with him: and Abram was seventy and five years old when he departed out of Haran.

5 And Abram took Sarai his wife, and Lot his brother's son, and all their substance that they had gathered, and the souls that they had gotten in Haran; and they went forth to go into the land of Canaan; and into the land of Canaan they came.

6 And Abram passed through the land unto the place of Sichem unto the plain of Moreh. And the Canaanite was then in the land.

7 And the LORD appeared unto Abram, and said, Unto thy seed will I give this land: and there builded he an altar unto the LORD, who appeared unto him.

8 And he removed from thence unto a mountain on the east of Beth-el, and pitched his tent, having Beth-el on the west, and Hai on the east: and there he builded an altar unto the LORD, and called upon the name of the LORD.

9 And Abram journeyed, going on still toward the south.

10 And there was a famine in the land: and Abram went down into Egypt to sojourn there; for the famine was grievous in the land.

11 And it came to pass, when he was come near to enter into Egypt, that he said unto Sarai his wife, Behold now, I know that thou art a fair woman to look upon:

12 Therefore it shall come to pass, when the Egyptians shall see thee, that they shall say, This is his wife: and they will kill me, but they will save thee alive.

13 Say, I pray thee, thou art my sister: that it may be well with me for thy sake; and my soul shall live because of thee.

14 And it came to pass, that, when Abram was come into Egypt, the Egyptians beheld the woman that she was very fair.

15 The princes also of Pharaoh saw her, and commended her before Pharaoh: and the woman was taken into Pharaoh's house.

16 And he entreated Abram well for her sake: and he had sheep, and oxen, and he asses, and menservants, and maidservants, and she asses, and camels.

17 And the LORD plagued Pharaoh and his house with great plagues because of Sarai Abram's wife.

18 And Pharaoh called Abram, and said, What is this that thou hast done unto me? Why didst thou not tell me that she was thy wife?

19 Why saidst thou, She is my sister? So I might have taken her to me to wife: now therefore behold thy wife, take her, and go thy way.

20 And Pharaoh commanded his men concerning him: and they sent him away, and his wife, and all that he had.

Summary

vv. 1–3

God calls Abram to go to a land that God will show him. God declares that He will bless Abram, make him a great nation, and make his name great. Abram will be a blessing, and God will bless those who bless Abram and curse those who curse him. Through Abram, all the families of the earth will be blessed.

vv. 4–9

Abram follows God's command and takes his wife and his nephew Lot with him. Abram is seventy-five years old at this time. They settle in Sichem on the plain of Moreh where the Canaanites live. God tells Abram that He will give Abram's seed this land, and Abram builds an altar to the Lord. Abram continues to call on the name of the Lord and continues to journey south.

vv. 10–15

There is a famine in the land, so Abram decides to go to Egypt. Because Sarai is attractive and the Egyptians might kill him to have her, Abram suggests that they should tell the Egyptians that Sarai is his sister. When they get to Egypt, Sarai is taken to Pharaoh's house because of her beauty.

vv. 16–20

The Egyptians treat Abram well because of Sarai, but God plagues Pharaoh because Sarai is in his house. Pharaoh confronts Abram and asks why he has deceived Pharaoh. Because of the deception, Pharaoh might have taken Sarai as a wife. Pharaoh commands them to leave, and they are sent away with all their possessions.

Commentary

In Genesis 12, God begins to focus on an individual man, Abram, and his family. It is through this covenant that the whole world will learn about God. Genesis 12:2 states, "I will make of thee a great nation, and I will bless thee, and make thy name great; and thou shalt be a blessing." God chooses to bless Abram so he can be a blessing to others. God is calling Abram into covenant with Him and establishing Abram's descendants as God's chosen people. God makes it clear that one of the results of this covenant is that Abram will be a blessing to others. Genesis 12:3 states, "And I will bless them that bless thee, and curse him that curseth thee: and in thee shall all families of the earth be blessed." This verse reemphasizes that God intends to bless all families of the earth through his covenant relationship with Abram. Although this chapter states a physical blessing of land to Abram's descendants, God is not just referring to a natural blessing of inheritance to Abram's descendants but to a spiritual blessing that all people will benefit from.

The covenant that God made with Abram is significant for relationship and redemption. When Adam sinned, the relationship that humanity had with God was broken. God wanted to reestablish the relationship, and that could only be done by redemption. Redemption means the release of people, animals, or property from bondage through the payment of a price. In this case, Jesus Christ redeemed humanity from the bondage of sin through the payment of his own life on Calvary and gave us the opportunity to reestablish our relationship with God.[42] But it was through Abram's descendants that Jesus Christ was born.

Even at this point in Abram's story, we see his faith. When God calls Abram, Abram already has an established inheritance from his father. God gives Abram

---

[42] Peter Lau, "Redemption," in *The Lexham Bible Dictionary*, eds. John D. Barry et al.

a choice of his current family's inheritance or an inheritance from the Lord. Abram has to be willing to give up his current inheritance that he can see for something which is promised.

Abram's great faith at the beginning of this chapter is in contrast to his lying to the Egyptians at the end of the chapter, which shows us that Abram does have faults. Despite the lie of Abram, God is faithful to His promise.

Review
1. What does the first verse of this chapter say about Abram's character and relationship with God?
2. How has verse 3 become a reality?
3. How is the covenant God makes with Abram related to redemption?
4. Why does Abram lie about Sarai being his wife? Do you believe he does not have faith in God?
5. Why does Pharaoh release Sarai back to Abram?

Genesis Chapter 13

1 *And Abram went up out of Egypt, he, and his wife, and all that he had, and Lot with him, into the south.*

2 And Abram was very rich in cattle, in silver, and in gold.

3 And he went on his journeys from the south even to Beth-el, unto the place where his tent had been at the beginning, between Beth-el and Hai;

4 Unto the place of the altar, which he had made there at the first: and there Abram called on the name of the LORD.

5 And Lot also, which went with Abram, had flocks, and herds, and tents.

6 And the land was not able to bear them, that they might dwell together: for their substance was great, so that they could not dwell together.

7 And there was a strife between the herdmen of Abram's cattle and the herdmen of Lot's cattle: and the Canaanite and the Perizzite dwelled then in the land.

8 And Abram said unto Lot, Let there be no strife, I pray thee, between me and thee, and between my herdmen and thy herdmen; for we be brethren.

9 Is not the whole land before thee? separate thyself, I pray thee, from me: if thou wilt take the left hand, then I will go to the right; or if thou depart to the right hand, then I will go to the left.

10 And Lot lifted up his eyes, and beheld all the plain of Jordan, that it was well watered every where, before the LORD destroyed Sodom and Gomorrah, even as the garden of the LORD, like the land of Egypt, as thou comest unto Zoar.

11 Then Lot chose him all the plain of Jordan; and Lot journeyed east: and they separated themselves the one from the other.

12 Abram dwelled in the land of Canaan, and Lot dwelled in the cities of the plain, and pitched his tent toward Sodom.

13 But the men of Sodom were wicked and sinners before the LORD exceedingly.

14 And the LORD said unto Abram, after that Lot was separated from him, Lift up now thine eyes, and look from the place where thou art northward, and southward, and eastward, and westward:

15 For all the land which thou seest, to thee will I give it, and to thy seed for ever.

16 And I will make thy seed as the dust of the earth: so that if a man can number the dust of the earth, then shall thy seed also be numbered.

17 Arise, walk through the land in the length of it and in the breadth of it; for I will give it unto thee.

18 Then Abram removed his tent, and came and dwelt in the plain of Mamre, which is in Hebron, and built there an altar unto the LORD.

Summary

vv. 1–7

Abram, his wife, and Lot leave Egypt and return to the place between Hai and Bethel, which is the place where Abram has built an altar and worshipped (Genesis 12:8). Both Abram and Lot have a large number of cattle, and the land cannot support all of them. Abram and Lot's herdsmen begin to argue over the land.

vv. 8–13

Abram and Lot divide their land. Abram gives Lot the choice of what land he wants to have. Lot chooses the land near Sodom and Gomorrah because it is more fertile, and he decides to live in the plain of Jordan near Sodom. The men of Sodom are wicked and sin before the Lord.

vv. 14–18

The Lord tells Abram that all the land he sees will be given to him and his descendants forever. He continues to bless Abram by stating that his descendants will be as many as the dust of the earth. God tells Abram to walk through the land because God is going to give it to him. Abram settles in Mamre and builds an altar to the Lord.

Commentary

In this chapter, Lot and Abram separate. When God spoke to Abram to leave his land and travel to Canaan, there is no record that God told Abram to bring Lot. Was it a mistake for Abram to bring Lot? In my opinion, Abram brought Lot because he was his closest relative and essentially his only heir because Sarai was barren. I believe that Lot was a hindrance to Abram because Lot still represented a tie with Abram's family and his "natural" inheritance.

Once Abram and Lot separate, God gives more details about Abram's blessing by saying that the blessing will include the land of Canaan and that he will have many descendants. Now that Abram has left his own land and left his family, he has to have faith in God that He will fulfill His promise because Abram has no natural way to make these things happen on his own.

Lot chooses the better land, which is fertile and well-watered. Lot's choice highlights his greed and Abram's unselfishness. Despite Lot's choice, God is faithful to His promise to Abram. It is God who brings His promises to pass, not man.

The author also mentions that the men of Sodom and Gomorrah are wicked and sinners, which foreshadows their destruction.

Review
1. What is the connection between Genesis 4:26 and Genesis 13:4?
2. When God called Abram, should Abram have brought Lot with him? What is your opinion?
3. What does Lot's choice say about his character?
4. In Genesis 13:14, is it significant that God restates Abram's blessing after he separates from Lot?
5. What is Genesis 13:13 a foreshadowing of?

Genesis Chapter 14

1 *And it came to pass in the days of Amraphel king of Shinar, Arioch king of Ellasar, Chedorlaomer king of Elam, and Tidal king of nations;*

2 That these made war with Bera king of Sodom, and with Birsha king of Gomorrah, Shinab king of Admah, and Shemeber king of Zeboiim, and the king of Bela, which is Zoar.

3 All these were joined together in the vale of Siddim, which is the salt sea.

4 Twelve years they served Chedorlaomer, and in the thirteenth year they rebelled.

5 And in the fourteenth year came Chedorlaomer, and the kings that were with him, and smote the Rephaims in Ashteroth Karnaim, and the Zuzims in Ham, and the Emims in Shaveh Kiriathaim,

6 And the Horites in their mount Seir, unto El-paran, which is by the wilderness.

7 And they returned, and came to En-mishpat, which is Kadesh, and smote all the country of the Amalekites, and also the Amorites, that dwelt in Hazezon-tamar.

8 And there went out the king of Sodom, and the king of Gomorrah, and the king of Admah, and the king of Zeboiim, and the king of Bela (the same is Zoar;) and they joined battle with them in the vale of Siddim;

9 With Chedorlaomer the king of Elam, and with Tidal king of nations, and Amraphel king of Shinar, and Arioch king of Ellasar; four kings with five.

10 And the vale of Siddim was full of slimepits; and the kings of Sodom and Gomorrah fled, and fell there; and they that remained fled to the mountain.

11 And they took all the goods of Sodom and Gomorrah, and all their victuals, and went their way.

12 And they took Lot, Abram's brother's son, who dwelt in Sodom, and his goods, and departed.

13 And there came one that had escaped, and told Abram the Hebrew; for he dwelt in the plain of Mamre the Amorite, brother of Eshcol, and brother of Aner: and these were confederate with Abram.

14 And when Abram heard that his brother was taken captive, he armed his trained servants, born in his own house, three hundred and eighteen, and pursued them unto Dan.

15 And he divided himself against them, he and his servants, by night, and smote them, and pursued them unto Hobah, which is on the left hand of Damascus.

16 And he brought back all the goods, and also brought again his brother Lot, and his goods, and the women also, and the people.

17 And the king of Sodom went out to meet him after his return from the slaughter of Chedorlaomer, and of the kings that were with him, at the valley of Shaveh, which is the king's dale.

18 And Melchizedek king of Salem brought forth bread and wine: and he was the priest of the most high God.

19 And he blessed him, and said, Blessed be Abram of the most high God, possessor of heaven and earth:

20 And blessed be the most high God, which hath delivered thine enemies into thy hand. And he gave him tithes of all.

21 And the king of Sodom said unto Abram, Give me the persons, and take the goods to thyself.

22 And Abram said to the king of Sodom, I have lift up mine hand unto the LORD, the most high God, the possessor of heaven and earth,

23 That I will not take from a thread even to a shoelatchet, and that I will not take any thing that is thine, lest thou shouldest say, I have made Abram rich:

24 Save only that which the young men have eaten, and the portion of the men which went with me, Aner, Eshcol, and Mamre; let them take their portion.

Summary

vv. 1–4

Amraphel, who is king of Shinar, Arioch, who is king of Ellasar, Chedorlaomer, who is king of Elam, and Tidal, who is king of Goyim, go to war against Bera, who is the king of Sodom, Birsha, who is king of Gomorrah, Shinab, who is king of Admah, Shemeber, who is king of Zeboiim, and the king of Bela, which is also called Zoar.

vv. 5–7
Chedorlaomer and his allies conquer the Rephaims, the Zuzims, the Emims, and the Horites. And they conquer the Amalekites.

vv. 8–12
Chedorlaomer and his allies fight against Sodom, Gomorrah, Zeboiim, and Bela, also called Zoar. The kings of Sodom and Gomorrah flee, and the four kings take their possessions and food. They also take Lot and his possessions because he lives in Sodom.

vv. 13–16
A man escapes and tells Abram what happened. Abram gathers 318 of his servants and goes to pursue the kings who have taken Lot. Abram is able to retrieve all that was taken and also saves Lot and his family.

vv. 17–24
After Abram defeats Chedorlaomer and the other kings, the king of Sodom comes to meet him. Then Melchizedek, who is the priest of the most high God, comes with bread and wine and blesses Abram. Abram gives him a tithe of everything, which is a tenth. The king of Sodom offers Abram the possessions he brings back from defeating the other kings, but Abram refuses. Abram states he made a promise to God that he will not take anything from the kings so they will not be able to say they made him rich. The only thing Abram accepts is what his men ate, and Abram's allies are allowed to accept their share of the spoil.

Commentary
Lot is taken into captivity as a consequence of a war that breaks out between kings in that area. Abram saves Lot from captivity. Lot's selfish choice places him in a vulnerable position, and he is still dependent on Abram for help. Despite his separation from Lot, Abram did the right thing by going to save Lot from captivity.

Abram does not accept the reward from the king of Sodom because he acknowledges that God is his source. He places his faith in God and not in man.

Abram pays a tithe to Melchizedek, acknowledging him as a priest of God. There is much speculation about Melchizedek, but for the purposes of this book, it is important that Abram recognizes him as a priest of God and pays a tithe to him. Many Christians still believe in paying tithes to God/church using this passage as support. (I am one of those Christians.)

Review
1. Why is Lot captured?
2. How is Abram informed about Lot's capture, and what is his response?
3. Who is Melchizedek, and why does Abram give him a tithe?
4. What is a tithe? Does the Bible support tithing today? If so, list some of these scriptures.
5. Why does Abram refuse any payment or gift from the king of Sodom?

Genesis Chapter 15

1 *After these things the word of the LORD came unto Abram in a vision, saying, Fear not, Abram: I am thy shield, and thy exceeding great reward. 2 And Abram said, Lord GOD, what wilt thou give me, seeing I go childless, and the steward of my house is this Eliezer of Damascus?*

3 And Abram said, Behold, to me thou hast given no seed: and, lo, one born in my house is mine heir.

4 And, behold, the word of the LORD came unto him, saying, This shall not be thine heir; but he that shall come forth out of thine own bowels shall be thine heir.

5 And he brought him forth abroad, and said, Look now toward heaven, and tell the stars, if thou be able to number them: and he said unto him, So shall thy seed be.

6 And he believed in the LORD; and he counted it to him for righteousness.

7 And he said unto him, I am the LORD that brought thee out of Ur of the Chaldees, to give thee this land to inherit it.

8 And he said, Lord GOD, whereby shall I know that I shall inherit it?

9 And he said unto him, Take me an heifer of three years old, and a she goat of three years old, and a ram of three years old, and a turtledove, and a young pigeon.

10 And he took unto him all these, and divided them in the midst, and laid each piece one against another: but the birds divided he not.

11 And when the fowls came down upon the carcases, Abram drove them away.

12 And when the sun was going down, a deep sleep fell upon Abram; and, lo, an horror of great darkness fell upon him.

13 And he said unto Abram, Know of a surety that thy seed shall be a stranger in a land that is not theirs, and shall serve them; and they shall afflict them four hundred years;

14 And also that nation, whom they shall serve, will I judge: and afterward shall they come out with great substance.

15 And thou shalt go to thy fathers in peace; thou shalt be buried in a good old age.

16 But in the fourth generation they shall come hither again: for the iniquity of the Amorites is not yet full.

17 And it came to pass, that, when the sun went down, and it was dark, behold a smoking furnace, and a burning lamp that passed between those pieces.

18 In the same day the LORD made a covenant with Abram, saying, Unto thy seed have I given this land, from the river of Egypt unto the great river, the river Euphrates:

19 The Kenites, and the Kenizzites, and the Kadmonites,

20 And the Hittites, and the Perizzites, and the Rephaims,

21 And the Amorites, and the Canaanites, and the Girgashites, and the Jebusites.

Summary

vv. 1–6

God speaks to Abram in a vision and states that God is Abram's shield and reward. Abram responds by stating that naturally he does not have an heir, and the steward of his house will be his heir. God clarifies that Abram's descendants will come from his natural offspring. God tells Abram that his descendants will be as many as the stars in the sky. Abram believes God, and he is considered righteous for his belief.

vv. 7–16

God identifies himself as the God that brought Abram out of Ur to the land of Chaldeans to inherit the land in which he now dwells. Abram asks how he will know that he will inherit it. God tells him to take a heifer that is three years old, a she-goat that is three years old, a ram that is three years old, a turtle dove, and a young pigeon. Abram divides the animals except for the birds and lays them down. Abram falls into a deep sleep and has a vision. In the vision, God tells Abram that his descendants will be strangers in a land and shall be afflicted for four hundred years. God will judge that nation, but the children of Israel will leave with great substance. In the fourth generation, they will return to this land of Canaan to inherit it.

vv. 17–21

When the sun goes down, Abram sees smoke passing between the divided animals. God reestablishes His covenant by stating that He is going to give Abram this land that the Kenites, Kenizzites, Kadmonites, Hittites, Perizzites, Rephaims, Amorites, Canaanites, Girgashites, and Jebusites now possess.

Commentary

God continues to reaffirm His covenant with Abram by stating that he will have many descendants from his own body. God uses vivid imagery of the stars to emphasize the multitude of Abram's descendants. Obviously, this is difficult to believe because Sarai is barren. Only by supernatural intervention can God keep His promise.

Genesis 15:6 is very significant. Paul discusses this verse in Romans and Galatians as to why faith is the basis of Christianity, even in the Old Testament. It is Abram's faith that makes him righteous. Righteousness means being in good standing with God.[43] So it is not any ritual he performs or any law that he keeps and obeys that makes him righteous. Abram's belief can be defined as "taking God at his word—believing that what he says will become a reality and then acting on that belief."[44]

Abram also does a ritual to establish this covenant. Abram is instructed to cut the animals in half, and when the sun goes down, Abram sees smoke moving between the divided animals. This is a familiar ritual that was performed during this time to establish a promise or a covenant.[45]

God also reveals to Abram some unpleasant news about the future of his descendants. His descendants will be servants in another land for four hundred years and then return to this land to inherit it. This refers to the Israelites in Egypt and their journey back to Canaan. This passage would obviously have been significant to Moses and the Israelites in their time because they were in the midst of fulfilling this prophecy. Although Abram will not see the total fulfillment of the blessing of land in his lifetime, he believes in God's promise.

---

[43] Michael F. Bird, "Righteousness," in *The Lexham Bible Dictionary,* eds. John D. Barry et al.

[44] Walton, *Genesis,* 421.

[45] Wenham, *Word Biblical Commentary,* 1:332–333.

Moses describes the geographical location of the Promised Land. It is important that the Israelites know what area God rightfully has promised them. Moses also presents a list of the people in the land, which is important to the original audience and for the modern reader. For the Israelites, they understood they were supposed to totally remove the inhabitants so they could possess the land. For the modern reader, we know that the Israelites did not totally remove the inhabitants as God had instructed them to do. Because the Israelites did not do as God instructed them, the Israelites constantly became influenced by pagan religions. They were eventually conquered and enslaved because they chose to serve other gods instead of the true God.

Review
1. Who does Abram suggest will be his heir because he is childless?
2. What metaphor is used in Genesis 15:5 to describe Abram's descendants?
3. Why is Genesis 15:6 significant to Christians today?
4. What event in the Israelite history is described in Genesis 15:13-14?
5. What is the significance of describing the geography of Abram's inherited land and the people living in it?

Genesis Chapter 16

1 Now Sarai Abram's wife bare him no children: and she had an handmaid, an Egyptian, whose name was Hagar.

2 And Sarai said unto Abram, Behold now, the LORD hath restrained me from bearing: I pray thee, go in unto my maid; it may be that I may obtain children by her. And Abram hearkened to the voice of Sarai.

3 And Sarai Abram's wife took Hagar her maid the Egyptian, after Abram had dwelt ten years in the land of Canaan, and gave her to her husband Abram to be his wife.

4 And he went in unto Hagar, and she conceived: and when she saw that she had conceived, her mistress was despised in her eyes.

5 And Sarai said unto Abram, My wrong be upon thee: I have given my maid into thy bosom; and when she saw that she had conceived, I was despised in her eyes: the LORD judge between me and thee.

6 But Abram said unto Sarai, Behold, thy maid is in thy hand; do to her as it pleaseth thee. And when Sarai dealt hardly with her, she fled from her face.

7 And the angel of the LORD found her by a fountain of water in the wilderness, by the fountain in the way to Shur.

8 And he said, Hagar, Sarai's maid, whence camest thou? and whither wilt thou go? And she said, I flee from the face of my mistress Sarai.

9 And the angel of the LORD said unto her, Return to thy mistress, and submit thyself under her hands.

10 And the angel of the LORD said unto her, I will multiply thy seed exceedingly, that it shall not be numbered for multitude.

11 And the angel of the LORD said unto her, Behold, thou art with child, and shalt bear a son, and shalt call his name Ishmael; because the LORD hath heard thy affliction.

12 And he will be a wild man; his hand will be against every man, and every man's hand against him; and he shall dwell in the presence of all his brethren.

13 And she called the name of the LORD that spake unto her, Thou God seest me: for she said, Have I also here looked after him that seeth me?

14 Wherefore the well was called Beer-lahai-roi; behold, it is between Kadesh and Bered.

15 And Hagar bare Abram a son: and Abram called his son's name, which Hagar bare, Ishmael.

16 And Abram was fourscore and six years old, when Hagar bare Ishmael to Abram.

Summary

vv. 1–6

It has been ten years, and Abram and Sarai still have no children. Sarai decides that she will give her servant Hagar to Abram as a second wife and have descendants by using her. Abram agrees and has sexual intercourse with Hagar, and she becomes pregnant. After Hagar becomes pregnant, she "despises" Sarah or looks down on her because she is barren. Abram tells Sarai that she can deal with Hagar however she wants. Sarai treats Hagar harshly, so she leaves.

vv. 7–14

Hagar leaves but is found by the angel of the Lord. The angel tells her to return and submit to Sarai. The angel states that God will multiply her descendants. She is told that she is going to have a son and to name him Ishmael. The angel says Ishmael will be a wild man.

vv. 15–16

Hagar gives birth to Ishmael. Abram is eighty-six years old.

Commentary

God confirms His covenant with Abram in chapter 15, but now it has been ten years since God originally promised Abram children. Although Sarai initiates the plan for Hagar to have a child with Abram, it appears that Abram has a lack of faith by agreeing to Sarai's plan. Although this concept is unacceptable to us today, it was the custom of this time for couples who had no children to have children by their servants and adopt them so their lineage would continue.[46] In the modern era, couples still use a surrogate if they cannot have children of their own, but the surrogate is usually impregnated by artificial means, and there is a contractual agreement to outline the rights and obligations of all parties. Despite the fact that Sarai's plan is successful, this is not God's plan. Sarai tries to take the place of God by manipulating the situation by her own means. God's divine blessing cannot be fulfilled by man's manipulation. Even though Sarai's plan works, it is not the fulfillment of the promise of God because *His* promise is only fulfilled by divine power.

Although Hagar is just an Egyptian servant, she has a significant experience with God because the angel of the Lord is sent to her. (*Hagar* means "to flee" or "flight.")[47] The angel gives Hagar instructions and informs her that she will have a son, and the angel gives him a name. This is the first time in the Bible that a prophecy is given about an individual before his or her birth. *Ishmael* means "who God hears."[48] Because Ishmael is the firstborn of Abram, God still promises to bless him. Ishmael is described as a "wild man," implying he will live a Bedouin life and not be easily tamed. The text also states, "His hand will be against every man, and every man's hand against him," which implies that his life of wandering and independence will put him in conflict with others.[49]

Hagar will also be blessed with many descendants that cannot be numbered. This is similar to the promise God gave to Abram. Essentially because of their relationship to Abram, who has a covenant blessing with God, both Hagar and Ishmael reap the benefits of similar blessings. This is one of the many ways we can see that all families of the earth will be blessed through Abram.

Review
1. What plan does Sarai have to produce an heir? Why do you think Abram agrees to the plan?
2. Why does Hagar flee from Sarai?
3. What is the significance of Hagar's and Ishmael's names?
4. What does God tell Hagar to do?
5. How is Hagar's blessing similar to Abram's blessing?

---

[46] Wenham, *Word Biblical Commentary*, 2:7.

[47] Michelle J. Morris, "Hagar," in *The Lexham Bible Dictionary,* eds. John D. Barry et al.

[48] The Holy Bible, King James Version (Grand Rapids: Zondervan, 2010).

[49] Wenham, *Word Biblical Commentary*, 2:11.

Genesis Chapter 17

1 *And when Abram was ninety years old and nine, the LORD appeared to Abram, and said unto him, I am the Almighty God; walk before me, and be thou perfect.*

2 And I will make my covenant between me and thee, and will multiply thee exceedingly.

3 And Abram fell on his face: and God talked with him, saying,

4 As for me, behold, my covenant is with thee, and thou shalt be a father of many nations.

5 Neither shall thy name any more be called Abram, but thy name shall be Abraham; for a father of many nations have I made thee.

6 And I will make thee exceeding fruitful, and I will make nations of thee, and kings shall come out of thee.

7 And I will establish my covenant between me and thee and thy seed after thee in their generations for an everlasting covenant, to be a God unto thee, and to thy seed after thee.

8 And I will give unto thee, and to thy seed after thee, the land wherein thou art a stranger, all the land of Canaan, for an everlasting possession; and I will be their God.

9 And God said unto Abraham, Thou shalt keep my covenant therefore, thou, and thy seed after thee in their generations.

10 This is my covenant, which ye shall keep, between me and you and thy seed after thee; Every man child among you shall be circumcised.

11 And ye shall circumcise the flesh of your foreskin; and it shall be a token of the covenant betwixt me and you.

12 And he that is eight days old shall be circumcised among you, every man child in your generations, he that is born in the house, or bought with money of any stranger, which is not of thy seed.

13 He that is born in thy house, and he that is bought with thy money, must needs be circumcised: and my covenant shall be in your flesh for an everlasting covenant.

14 And the uncircumcised man child whose flesh of his foreskin is not circumcised, that soul shall be cut off from his people; he hath broken my covenant.

15 And God said unto Abraham, As for Sarai thy wife, thou shalt not call her name Sarai, but Sarah shall her name be.

16 And I will bless her, and give thee a son also of her: yea, I will bless her, and she shall be a mother of nations; kings of people shall be of her.

17 Then Abraham fell upon his face, and laughed, and said in his heart, Shall a child be born unto him that is an hundred years old? and shall Sarah, that is ninety years old, bear?

18 And Abraham said unto God, O that Ishmael might live before thee!

19 And God said, Sarah thy wife shall bear thee a son indeed; and thou shalt call his name Isaac: and I will establish my covenant with him for an everlasting covenant, and with his seed after him.

20 And as for Ishmael, I have heard thee: Behold, I have blessed him, and will make him fruitful, and will multiply him exceedingly; twelve princes shall he beget, and I will make him a great nation.

21 But my covenant will I establish with Isaac, which Sarah shall bear unto thee at this set time in the next year.

22 And he left off talking with him, and God went up from Abraham.

23 And Abraham took Ishmael his son, and all that were born in his house, and all that were bought with his money, every male among the men of Abraham's house; and circumcised the flesh of their foreskin in the selfsame day, as God had said unto him.

24 And Abraham was ninety years old and nine, when he was circumcised in the flesh of his foreskin.

25 And Ishmael his son was thirteen years old, when he was circumcised in the flesh of his foreskin.

26 In the selfsame day was Abraham circumcised, and Ishmael his son.

27 And all the men of his house, born in the house, and bought with money of the stranger, were circumcised with him.

Summary

vv. 1–5

Abram is now ninety-nine years old, and God reaffirms His covenant with Abram. Abram falls on his face as God speaks to him, and God tells Abram he will be the father of many nations. Abram's name (*Abram* means "exalted father")[50] is changed to Abraham.

vv. 6–8

God not only states that Abraham will have a multitude of descendants, but He also adds that some of Abraham's descendants will be kings and many nations will come from him. God once again reestablishes His promise of land to Abraham's descendants.

vv. 9–14

God institutes a physical sign for the covenant that He establishes with Abraham. The sign is circumcision. Every male in Abraham's house, including servants, must be circumcised. On the eighth day after the birth of a baby boy, he must be circumcised, and this includes all of Abraham's descendants.

vv. 15–16

God changes Sarai's name to Sarah. God also states that Sarah will have a son and that she will be the mother of kings and of many nations.

vv. 17–19

Abraham's initial response is laughter. He asks how he, at one hundred years old, and Sarah, at ninety years old, can have a child. God replies by stating that Sarah will have a son, and his name will be Isaac. The covenant that God is establishing with Abraham is going to be fulfilled by Isaac and his descendants.

v. 20

God will bless Ishmael and multiply his descendants. He will be the father of twelve princes.

vv. 21–22

God restates that His covenant will be through Isaac, and Sarah will give birth to him the next year.

---

[50] Longman, *How to Read Genesis*, 132.

vv. 23–27

Abraham obeys God's command. He is circumcised at ninety-nine years old. Ishmael is circumcised at thirteen years old. All the men of Abraham's house are circumcised.

Commentary

The last chapter ended with the birth of Ishmael when Abram was eighty-six years old, and this chapter begins with Abram at ninety-nine years old. It has been thirteen years since there is any record that God spoke to Abram.

God changes Abraham and Sarah's names, which is significant. For example, traditionally in marriage, a woman changes her last name to the last name of her husband to symbolize that she is no longer bound to her birth family but is bound to her husband as a new unit. The symbolism is similar here. Abraham and Sarah are not bound to their old life before Abraham knew God but are now bound to God. As husband and wife, Abraham and Sarah are one in the eyes of God, so they both are blessed as being the father and mother of a multitude. *Abraham* means "the father of a multitude," and *Sarah* means "princess."[51]

There is spiritual significance to Abraham's changed name. When he was called Abram, he became the father of Ishmael, but when his name was changed to Abraham, he became the father of Isaac. The name of his natural family produced a natural son, but the name that God gave Abraham produced a supernatural son.

In verse 9, God states that Abraham will keep the covenant. The modern reader usually thinks of the Old Testament laws as the covenant, but the Mosaic laws had not been established at this time. Keeping the covenant for Abraham is his obedience, his faithfulness, and his belief in God. The only sign God establishes with Abraham at this time is circumcision. The sign of circumcision is important to both Christians and Jews. In Christianity, we believe that obedience, faithfulness, and belief in God are how we establish and continue to grow in our relationship with God. Although we are no longer required to do the natural act of circumcision, we are circumcised in the heart and spirit.[52] (In the Jewish tradition, a baby boy is still circumcised on the eighth day, and this is called *brit milah*.)[53]

When Ishmael was born, Abraham probably thought he was the son who God had promised. It is not until this chapter, thirteen years later, that God states that

---

[51] The Holy Bible, King James Version (Grand Rapids: Zondervan, 2010).
[52] Deuteronomy 30:6, Romans 2:29
[53] "Brit Milah," Wikipedia, last modified August 25, 2022, https://en.wikipedia.org/wiki/Brit_milah.

Sarah will have a son. In this chapter, not only does God promise to bless Abraham with many descendants, but He also promises to bless Sarah with many descendants. Although I am sure Abraham is overjoyed that he and his wife will be parents, he is saddened because he loves Ishmael. Although God's covenant blessing will be established through Isaac, God promises to bless Ishmael and his descendants because he is Abraham's son.

Review
1. How long has it been from the end of chapter 16 to the beginning of chapter 17?
2. What are Abram and Sarai's names changed to? Discuss the meaning and relevance of the new names.
3. What is the physical sign of the covenant God makes with Abraham? Is it still practiced today? Is it still a sign of the covenant that God made with Abraham?
4. What is Abraham's response to God telling him that Sarah will have a child?
5. What is the blessing that God gives Ishmael? How is this related to Abraham's blessing?

Genesis Chapter 18

1 *And the LORD appeared unto him in the plains of Mamre: and he sat in the tent door in the heat of the day;*

2 And he lift up his eyes and looked, and, lo, three men stood by him: and when he saw them, he ran to meet them from the tent door, and bowed himself toward the ground,

3 And said, My Lord, if now I have found favour in thy sight, pass not away, I pray thee, from thy servant:

4 Let a little water, I pray you, be fetched, and wash your feet, and rest yourselves under the tree:

5 And I will fetch a morsel of bread, and comfort ye your hearts; after that ye shall pass on: for therefore are ye come to your servant. And they said, So do, as thou hast said.

6 And Abraham hastened into the tent unto Sarah, and said, Make ready quickly three measures of fine meal, knead it, and make cakes upon the hearth.

7 And Abraham ran unto the herd, and fetcht a calf tender and good, and gave it unto a young man; and he hasted to dress it.

8 And he took butter, and milk, and the calf which he had dressed, and set it before them; and he stood by them under the tree, and they did eat.

9 And they said unto him, Where is Sarah thy wife? And he said, Behold, in the tent.

10 And he said, I will certainly return unto thee according to the time of life; and, lo, Sarah thy wife shall have a son. And Sarah heard it in the tent door, which was behind him.

11 Now Abraham and Sarah were old and well stricken in age; and it ceased to be with Sarah after the manner of women.

12 Therefore Sarah laughed within herself, saying, After I am waxed old shall I have pleasure, my lord being old also?

13 And the LORD said unto Abraham, Wherefore did Sarah laugh, saying, Shall I of a surety bear a child, which am old?

14 Is any thing too hard for the LORD? At the time appointed I will return unto thee, according to the time of life, and Sarah shall have a son.

15 Then Sarah denied, saying, I laughed not; for she was afraid. And he said, Nay; but thou didst laugh.

16 And the men rose up from thence, and looked toward Sodom: and Abraham went with them to bring them on the way.

17 And the LORD said, Shall I hide from Abraham that thing which I do;

18 Seeing that Abraham shall surely become a great and mighty nation, and all the nations of the earth shall be blessed in him?

19 For I know him, that he will command his children and his household after him, and they shall keep the way of the LORD, to do justice and judgment; that the LORD may bring upon Abraham that which he hath spoken of him.

20 And the LORD said, Because the cry of Sodom and Gomorrah is great, and because their sin is very grievous;

21 I will go down now, and see whether they have done altogether according to the cry of it, which is come unto me; and if not, I will know.

22 And the men turned their faces from thence, and went toward Sodom: but Abraham stood yet before the LORD.

23 And Abraham drew near, and said, Wilt thou also destroy the righteous with the wicked?

24 Peradventure there be fifty righteous within the city: wilt thou also destroy and not spare the place for the fifty righteous that are therein?

25 That be far from thee to do after this manner, to slay the righteous with the wicked: and that the righteous should be as the wicked, that be far from thee: Shall not the Judge of all the earth do right?

26 And the LORD said, If I find in Sodom fifty righteous within the city, then I will spare all the place for their sakes.

27 And Abraham answered and said, Behold now, I have taken upon me to speak unto the Lord, which am but dust and ashes:

28 Peradventure there shall lack five of the fifty righteous: wilt thou destroy all the city for lack of five? And he said, If I find there forty and five, I will not destroy it.

29 And he spake unto him yet again, and said, Peradventure there shall be forty found there. And he said, I will not do it for forty's sake.

30 And he said unto him, Oh let not the Lord be angry, and I will speak: Peradventure there shall thirty be found there. And he said, I will not do it, if I find thirty there.

31 And he said, Behold now, I have taken upon me to speak unto the Lord: Peradventure there shall be twenty found there. And he said, I will not destroy it for twenty's sake.

32 And he said, Oh let not the Lord be angry, and I will speak yet but this once: Peradventure ten shall be found there. And he said, I will not destroy it for ten's sake.

33 And the LORD went his way, as soon as he had left communing with Abraham: and Abraham returned unto his place.

Summary
vv. 1–8
The author identifies the three visitors as "Lord." Abraham greets them as the Lord. He brings them water to wash their feet. He offers them food and tells Sarah to prepare cakes for them. Abraham also prepares a young calf for them and gives them milk to drink.

vv. 9–10
The visitors ask about Sarah, and Abraham replies that she is in the tent. Then the visitors restate what God told Abraham in the previous chapter, that Sarah will have a son at this time next year.

vv. 11–12
Abraham and Sarah are both elderly. Sarah is postmenopausal and physically unable to have children. Sarah overhears this conversation and laughs. She asks, after she and her husband are old, would they now have the pleasure of having a child?

vv. 13–15
The Lord asks why Sarah laughed. The Lord responds to His own question by saying nothing is too hard for Him. At this time next year, Sarah will have a son. Sarah denies that she laughed because she is afraid, but she did laugh.

vv. 16–21

The three visitors start to travel toward Sodom. God knows that Abraham is faithful, obedient, and that he will do what is just and right. Because of Abraham's relationship with God and the covenant God has made with him, God considers telling Abraham of his plans for Sodom and Gomorrah. The Lord states to Abraham that the sin of Sodom and Gomorrah is great, and the Lord will dispense judgment.

vv. 23–33

Abraham discusses with God the possibility of saving the cities for a small number of righteous people. Abraham starts off at fifty people and ends with ten. God does agree to save the cities for ten righteous people.

Commentary

In this passage, the Lord takes the form of three men. This is called a theophany. A theophany is a visual manifestation to humanity of God.[54] The visitors speak to Abraham as if their words are directly from God. Although the visitors are three men, they speak as one voice from the Lord. The important point here is that the message Abraham is receiving comes directly from God.

Almost every time there is a prophecy about Abraham and Sarah having children, there is also a mention of their age and that Sarah is past the age to be able to have children naturally. This is emphasized so that we must never forget that it is God who will fulfill the promise, not human manipulation.

Sarah's laugh is similar to Abraham's in the previous chapter. Does Abraham tell Sarah what God told him in chapter 17? Her response is as if she is hearing it for the first time. *Isaac* means "laughter."[55] Abraham and Sarah's response to Isaac's birth is a foreshadowing of his name.

This chapter ends with God's discussion with Abraham about the judgment of Sodom and Gomorrah. God has such love and respect for Abraham that He talks to Abraham like a true friend. Because of God's love and compassion for mankind, He is willing to save the entire city for ten righteous people. The numbers are not necessarily important, but the significance is that God is just and will not destroy the cities for the sake of even a small number of righteous people.

---

[54] Matthew D. Montonini, "Theophany," in *The Lexham Bible Dictionary*, eds. John D. Barry et al.

[55] Sailhamer, "Genesis," in *The Expositor's Bible Commentary*, 140.

Review
1. Why does Abraham address the three men as Lord?
2. What does the Lord tell Abraham will happen to Sarah?
3. What is Sarah's response to what the Lord says? Compare her response to Abraham's response in the previous chapter.
4. Why does the Lord tell Abraham His plan for Sodom and Gomorrah?
5. What is the number of righteous people that will have to be found in Sodom for the Lord not to destroy it?

Genesis Chapter 19

1   *And there came two angels to Sodom at even; and Lot sat in the gate of Sodom: and Lot seeing them rose up to meet them; and he bowed himself with his face toward the ground;*

2 And he said, Behold now, my lords, turn in, I pray you, into your servant's house, and tarry all night, and wash your feet, and ye shall rise up early, and go on your ways. And they said, Nay; but we will abide in the street all night.

3 And he pressed upon them greatly; and they turned in unto him, and entered into his house; and he made them a feast, and did bake unleavened bread, and they did eat.

4 But before they lay down, the men of the city, even the men of Sodom, compassed the house round, both old and young, all the people from every quarter:

5 And they called unto Lot, and said unto him, Where are the men which came in to thee this night? bring them out unto us, that we may know them.

6 And Lot went out at the door unto them, and shut the door after him,

7 And said, I pray you, brethren, do not so wickedly.

8 Behold now, I have two daughters which have not known man; let me, I pray you, bring them out unto you, and do ye to them as is good in your eyes: only unto these men do nothing; for therefore came they under the shadow of my roof.

9 And they said, Stand back. And they said again, This one fellow came in to sojourn, and he will needs be a judge: now will we deal worse with thee, than with them. And they pressed sore upon the man, even Lot, and came near to break the door.

10 But the men put forth their hand, and pulled Lot into the house to them, and shut to the door.

11 And they smote the men that were at the door of the house with blindness, both small and great: so that they wearied themselves to find the door.

12 And the men said unto Lot, Hast thou here any besides? son in law, and thy sons, and thy daughters, and whatsoever thou hast in the city, bring them out of this place:

13 For we will destroy this place, because the cry of them is waxen great before the face of the LORD; and the LORD hath sent us to destroy it.

14 And Lot went out, and spake unto his sons in law, which married his daughters, and said, Up, get you out of this place; for the LORD will destroy this city. But he seemed as one that mocked unto his sons in law.

15 And when the morning arose, then the angels hastened Lot, saying, Arise, take thy wife, and thy two daughters, which are here; lest thou be consumed in the iniquity of the city.

16 And while he lingered, the men laid hold upon his hand, and upon the hand of his wife, and upon the hand of his two daughters; the LORD being merciful unto him: and they brought him forth, and set him without the city.

17 And it came to pass, when they had brought them forth abroad, that he said, Escape for thy life; look not behind thee, neither stay thou in all the plain; escape to the mountain, lest thou be consumed.

18 And Lot said unto them, Oh, not so, my Lord:

19 Behold now, thy servant hath found grace in thy sight, and thou hast magnified thy mercy, which thou hast shewed unto me in saving my life; and I cannot escape to the mountain, lest some evil take me, and I die:

20 Behold now, this city is near to flee unto, and it is a little one: Oh, let me escape thither, (is it not a little one?) and my soul shall live.

21 And he said unto him, See, I have accepted thee concerning this thing also, that I will not overthrow this city, for the which thou hast spoken.

22 Haste thee, escape thither; for I cannot do any thing till thou be come thither. Therefore the name of the city was called Zoar.

23 The sun was risen upon the earth when Lot entered into Zoar.

24 Then the LORD rained upon Sodom and upon Gomorrah brimstone and fire from the LORD out of heaven;

25 And he overthrew those cities, and all the plain, and all the inhabitants of the cities, and that which grew upon the ground.

26 But his wife looked back from behind him, and she became a pillar of salt.

27 And Abraham gat up early in the morning to the place where he stood before the LORD:

28 And he looked toward Sodom and Gomorrah, and toward all the land of the plain, and beheld, and, lo, the smoke of the country went up as the smoke of a furnace.

29 And it came to pass, when God destroyed the cities of the plain, that God remembered Abraham, and sent Lot out of the midst of the overthrow, when he overthrew the cities in the which Lot dwelt.

30 And Lot went up out of Zoar, and dwelt in the mountain, and his two daughters with him; for he feared to dwell in Zoar: and he dwelt in a cave, he and his two daughters.

31 And the firstborn said unto the younger, Our father is old, and there is not a man in the earth to come in unto us after the manner of all the earth:

32 Come, let us make our father drink wine, and we will lie with him, that we may preserve seed of our father.

33 And they made their father drink wine that night: and the firstborn went in, and lay with her father; and he perceived not when she lay down, nor when she arose.

34 And it came to pass on the morrow, that the firstborn said unto the younger, Behold, I lay yesternight with my father: let us make him drink wine this night also; and go thou in, and lie with him, that we may preserve seed of our father.

35 And they made their father drink wine that night also: and the younger arose, and lay with him; and he perceived not when she lay down, nor when she arose.

36 Thus were both the daughters of Lot with child by their father.

37 And the firstborn bare a son, and called his name Moab: the same is the father of the Moabites unto this day.

38 And the younger, she also bare a son, and called his name Ben-ammi: the same is the father of the children of Ammon unto this day.

Summary

vv. 1–3

Lot is visited by two angels and greets them at the city gate. He washes their feet and offers them a place to stay for the night. At first, they say they would prefer to stay out in the street all night, but Lot persuades them to come to his house and makes them a feast.

vv. 4–7

Before they are able to lie down to go to sleep, the men of the city, which include both young and old men, surround Lot's house and demand that the two men come out so they can have sex with them. Lot pleads with them not to act so wickedly.

vv. 8–14

Lot offers his two daughters to the men of Sodom instead. They respond by stating that he is a stranger in their city, yet he judges their actions. They continue to state they will deal worse with Lot than they plan to do with the two visitors and attempt to attack Lot. But the visitors pull Lot inside, and his daughters are not given to the men of Sodom. The visitors (angels) blind the men, and they can no longer find the door. The angels ask Lot if he has any other family members who are not in the house because they are going to destroy Sodom because of the sin. Lot goes and speaks with his daughters' fiancés, but they do not believe him and make fun of him.

vv. 15–23

The next morning, the angels attempt to rush Lot to leave, but he lingers. The angels hold the hand of Lot, his wife, and his daughters and bring them out of the city. When they are out of the city, the angels tell Lot and his family not to look back and to go into the mountains. Lot requests to go to a small city called Zoar instead. So Lot goes to Zoar.

vv. 24–26

The Lord destroys Sodom and Gomorrah and the other cities on the plain. But Lot's wife looks back and becomes a pillar of salt.

vv. 27–29

Abraham gets up early and goes to the place where he had heard from the Lord. He looks toward Sodom and Gomorrah and sees the smoke of the city burning. God remembers Abraham, and that is why Lot's family is allowed to leave and go to Zoar.

vv. 30–38

Lot and his daughters leave Zoar and settle in the mountains. Lot's daughters decide to have sex with him to produce heirs because there are no available men. The oldest daughter gets Lot drunk and has sex with him, and the younger daughter does the same thing. Both times, Lot does not know what has happened. The oldest daughter has a son named Moab, and he becomes the father of the

Moabites. The youngest daughter has a son named Ben-ammi, and he becomes the father of the Ammonites.

Commentary

In this chapter, we have another example of theophany where the two angels represented the Lord. Not only do they protect Lot and his family, they literally take them by the hand and lead them out of Sodom. Although Sodom and Gomorrah have widespread sin, it appears that Lot tries to have a positive influence by attempting to convince the men of Sodom not to assault the angels.

Lot's actions in this chapter in addition to his previous behavior call his character into question. Lot's choice of moving to Sodom seemed selfish because he chose the land that was well-watered for himself. In this chapter, he offers his virgin daughters to the men in the city instead of giving them the angels. Although one might understand him trying to protect the angels, this action reveals a serious character flaw. Lot also seems to be attached to Sodom, which was extremely evil, in that he had to be dragged out by the angels. In my opinion, he is attached to the immoral behavior in the city. His wife turning toward the city implies that she is so attached that she has to look back.

The chapter ends with the incest between Lot and his daughters. The fact that the daughters plotted to get him drunk implies that Lot would not have agreed to their plan if he were sober. The first daughter has a son called Moab, who is the father of the Moabites. The second daughter has a son called Ben-ammi, who is the father of the Ammonites. The Moabites and Ammonites were distant relatives of the Israelites and often were in conflict with the Israelites throughout the Old Testament.

The destruction of Sodom and Gomorrah is often used to condemn homosexuality. Sodom and Gomorrah had widespread sin including homosexuality. Although homosexuality is a sin and abomination, the people of Sodom and Gomorrah had turned from God and had allowed their hearts to be hardened, and as a result, they participated in every type of sin, and this is why God destroyed them.

Review

1. Are Lot's two visitors men or angels?
2. Why does Lot offer his daughters to the men in Sodom?
3. What plan do Lot's daughters devise once they settle in the mountains?
4. What are the names of the two nations that Lot and his daughters produced?
5. What do Lot's actions in this chapter say about his character?

Genesis Chapter 20

1 *And Abraham journeyed from thence toward the south country, and dwelled between Kadesh and Shur, and sojourned in Gerar.*

2 And Abraham said of Sarah his wife, She is my sister: and Abimelech king of Gerar sent, and took Sarah.

3 But God came to Abimelech in a dream by night, and said to him, Behold, thou art but a dead man, for the woman which thou hast taken; for she is a man's wife.

4 But Abimelech had not come near her: and he said, Lord, wilt thou slay also a righteous nation?

5 Said he not unto me, She is my sister? and she, even she herself said, He is my brother: in the integrity of my heart and innocency of my hands have I done this.

6 And God said unto him in a dream, Yea, I know that thou didst this in the integrity of thy heart; for I also withheld thee from sinning against me: therefore suffered I thee not to touch her.

7 Now therefore restore the man his wife; for he is a prophet, and he shall pray for thee, and thou shalt live: and if thou restore her not, know thou that thou shalt surely die, thou, and all that are thine.

8 Therefore Abimelech rose early in the morning, and called all his servants, and told all these things in their ears: and the men were sore afraid.

9 Then Abimelech called Abraham, and said unto him, What hast thou done unto us? and what have I offended thee, that thou hast brought on me and on my kingdom a great sin? thou hast done deeds unto me that ought not to be done.

10 And Abimelech said unto Abraham, What sawest thou, that thou hast done this thing?

11 And Abraham said, Because I thought, Surely the fear of God is not in this place; and they will slay me for my wife's sake.

12 And yet indeed she is my sister; she is the daughter of my father, but not the daughter of my mother; and she became my wife.

13 And it came to pass, when God caused me to wander from my father's house, that I said unto her, This is thy kindness which thou shalt shew unto me; at every place whither we shall come, say of me, He is my brother.

14 And Abimelech took sheep, and oxen, and menservants, and womenservants, and gave them unto Abraham, and restored him Sarah his wife.

15 And Abimelech said, Behold, my land is before thee: dwell where it pleaseth thee.

16 And unto Sarah he said, Behold, I have given thy brother a thousand pieces of silver: behold, he is to thee a covering of the eyes, unto all that are with thee, and with all other: thus she was reproved.

17 So Abraham prayed unto God: and God healed Abimelech, and his wife, and his maidservants; and they bare children.

18 For the LORD had fast closed up all the wombs of the house of Abimelech, because of Sarah Abraham's wife.

Summary

vv. 1–2

Abraham and Sarah go to the land of Gerar, and again, they say that Sarah is Abraham's sister.

vv. 3–7

God comes to Abimelech in a dream and tells him to restore Sarah back to Abraham because she is his wife. Abimelech replies by stating he has done nothing wrong because he was deceived. God replies that because he was deceived, God is giving him the opportunity to restore Sarah to Abraham.

vv. 8–13

Abimelech approaches Abraham and asks why he deceived him. Abraham states that Sarah is his half-sister because they have the same father. Abraham reveals that he asked Sarah to say that she was his sister because he believed that the people had no respect for God and would kill him for his wife.

vv. 14–18

Abimelech restores Sarah and gives Abraham servants and cattle as gifts. He uses the term "brother" in reference to Abraham, which acknowledges what Abraham has told him about Sarah being Abraham's half-sister. Abraham then prays for him, and the Lord lifts the curse of infertility from Abimelech, his servants, and his wives.

Commentary

Abraham lied twice about Sarah being his wife. Abraham's lies seem such a contrast to the way he has been portrayed as being a great man of faith. Abraham has faith to believe in all of God's promises, yet is fearful that God will not protect him. Despite Abraham's faith, this is an example of his human frailty and that he does make mistakes.

This is the first time someone is referred to as a prophet. Abraham is referred to as a prophet to Abimelech. Even at that time, prophets were considered people who were special to God and could proclaim blessings.[56] Despite the fact that Abraham lies and causes Abimelech's household to be barren, Abimelech gives Abraham gifts and restores Sarah to Abraham. Abraham fulfills his title as prophet by praying for Abimelech and lifting the curse of infertility from his household.

Review
1. Besides being husband and wife, how else are Abraham and Sarah related?
2. How does Abimelech discover that Abraham and Sarah deceived him?
3. What did the Lord do to all the women in the house of Abimelech because he took Sarah to be his wife?
4. What does Abraham do for Abimelech before they leave?
5. What are the similarities and differences in Abraham's and Sarah's actions in this chapter compared to chapter 12?

---

[56] Walton, *Genesis*, 495.

Genesis Chapter 21

1   *And the LORD visited Sarah as he had said, and the LORD did unto Sarah as he had spoken.*

2 For Sarah conceived, and bare Abraham a son in his old age, at the set time of which God had spoken to him.

3 And Abraham called the name of his son that was born unto him, whom Sarah bare to him, Isaac.

4 And Abraham circumcised his son Isaac being eight days old, as God had commanded him.

5 And Abraham was an hundred years old, when his son Isaac was born unto him.

6 And Sarah said, God hath made me to laugh, so that all that hear will laugh with me.

7 And she said, Who would have said unto Abraham, that Sarah should have given children suck? for I have born him a son in his old age.

8 And the child grew, and was weaned: and Abraham made a great feast the same day that Isaac was weaned.

9 And Sarah saw the son of Hagar the Egyptian, which she had born unto Abraham, mocking.

10 Wherefore she said unto Abraham, Cast out this bondwoman and her son: for the son of this bondwoman shall not be heir with my son, even with Isaac.

11 And the thing was very grievous in Abraham's sight because of his son.

12 And God said unto Abraham, Let it not be grievous in thy sight because of the lad, and because of thy bondwoman; in all that Sarah hath said unto thee, hearken unto her voice; for in Isaac shall thy seed be called.

13 And also of the son of the bondwoman will I make a nation, because he is thy seed.

14 And Abraham rose up early in the morning, and took bread, and a bottle of water, and gave it unto Hagar, putting it on her shoulder, and the child, and sent her away: and she departed, and wandered in the wilderness of Beer-sheba.

15 And the water was spent in the bottle, and she cast the child under one of the shrubs.

16 And she went, and sat her down over against him a good way off, as it were a bowshot: for she said, Let me not see the death of the child. And she sat over against him, and lift up her voice, and wept.

17 And God heard the voice of the lad; and the angel of God called to Hagar out of heaven, and said unto her, What aileth thee, Hagar? fear not; for God hath heard the voice of the lad where he is.

18 Arise, lift up the lad, and hold him in thine hand; for I will make him a great nation.

19 And God opened her eyes, and she saw a well of water; and she went, and filled the bottle with water, and gave the lad drink.

20 And God was with the lad; and he grew, and dwelt in the wilderness, and became an archer.

21 And he dwelt in the wilderness of Paran: and his mother took him a wife out of the land of Egypt.

22 And it came to pass at that time, that Abimelech and Phichol the chief captain of his host spake unto Abraham, saying, God is with thee in all that thou doest:

23 Now therefore swear unto me here by God that thou wilt not deal falsely with me, nor with my son, nor with my son's son: but according to the kindness that I have done unto thee, thou shalt do unto me, and to the land wherein thou hast sojourned.

24 And Abraham said, I will swear.

25 And Abraham reproved Abimelech because of a well of water, which Abimelech's servants had violently taken away.

26 And Abimelech said, I wot not who hath done this thing: neither didst thou tell me, neither yet heard I of it, but to day.

27 And Abraham took sheep and oxen, and gave them unto Abimelech; and both of them made a covenant.

28 And Abraham set seven ewe lambs of the flock by themselves.

29 And Abimelech said unto Abraham, What mean these seven ewe lambs which thou hast set by themselves?

30 And he said, For these seven ewe lambs shalt thou take of my hand, that they may be a witness unto me, that I have digged this well.

31 Wherefore he called that place Beer-sheba; because there they sware both of them.

32 Thus they made a covenant at Beer-sheba: then Abimelech rose up, and Phichol the chief captain of his host, and they returned into the land of the Philistines.

33 And Abraham planted a grove in Beer-sheba, and called there on the name of the LORD, the everlasting God.

34 And Abraham sojourned in the Philistines' land many days.

Summary

vv. 1–4

Sarah has a son and names him Isaac just as God has said. Isaac is circumcised by Abraham on the eighth day just as God commanded.

vv. 5–7

Abraham is one hundred years old when Isaac is born. Sarah says that God has made her laugh and asks who would have said that she and Abraham would have a child in their old age.

vv. 8–14

Once Isaac is weaned, Abraham throws a feast for him. Sarah sees Ishmael mocking Isaac. Sarah no longer wants Hagar and Ishmael around, so she asks Abraham to make them leave. God tells him to follow Sarah's advice. This saddens Abraham because Ishmael is his son also, but God says that He will make Ishmael a great nation. Abraham gives Hagar and Ishmael bread and water and sends them into the wilderness.

vv 15–21

Hagar and Ishmael run out of water and food. Hagar sits and rests a distance away from Ishmael because she does not want to watch her son die. God hears Ishmael's voice crying out. God tells Hagar He heard Ishmael's voice and that He is going to make Ishmael into a great nation. Then she opens her eyes and sees a well of water, and they both begin to drink. Ishmael settles in the wilderness of Paran and Hagar takes a wife from Egypt for Ishmael.

vv. 22–24

Abraham is approached by Abimelech and Phichol, who is the captain of Abimelech's army. They ask him to swear to them that Abraham will treat Abimelech and his descendants fairly. Abraham says that he will.

vv. 25–34

Abraham complains to Abimelech that his servants have taken one of his wells. Abimelech responds that he does not know about this. Abraham gives Abimelech sheep and oxen and makes a covenant with him. Then Abraham takes seven ewe lambs and sets them apart. Abimelech asks about the purpose of the lambs. Abraham replies by stating that he is giving Abimelech these seven lambs as a witness that Abraham dug this well. They name the area Beer-sheba and make a covenant there. Abimelech and Phicol return to the land of the Philistines. Abraham plants a grove there and calls on the name of the Lord. He lives in the land of the Philistines for a long time.

Commentary

The description of Isaac's birth is very anticlimactic considering all the promises and time that led up to this point. "At the appointed time" references the promises of chapters 17 and 18, which is evidence that God is faithful and fulfills His promise at the time promised.

Once again, the ages of Abraham and Sarah are emphasized. Because of their old age, we understand that it is God who has performed this miracle. Isaac is not born by natural human means. *Isaac* means "laughter" because Abraham laughed when God told him that Sarah was going to have a son. Sarah also laughed when she was told that she was going to have a son, and laughter is mentioned again in this chapter.

Now that Isaac is born, there is conflict between the two sons. Ishmael has to leave because he is an obstacle to Isaac's being able to have his full inheritance. Although God blesses Ishmael, the covenant is fulfilled through Isaac. Isaac's descendants consider themselves superior to all their distant relatives because they are God's chosen people. This concept is seen throughout the Bible. The Israelites continue to be in conflict with the Ishmaelites, Moabites, Ammonites, Midianites, and Edomites, which are all distant relatives of the Israelites.

Hagar leaves again, which is similar to when she fled in chapter 16. *Hagar* means "to flee." Hagar is one of the few people who have two experiences with God, though she is not one of the "chosen" people.

There are several parts to the covenant that God makes with Abraham. God says He is going to make Abraham's name great, that he would have many descendants, and that he would have the land of Canaan. Although the beginning of one of the parts is fulfilled with the birth of Isaac, Abraham does not possess the land that is promised to him. At this point, Abraham is still living with the Philistines in the land of Canaan (the Promised Land).

Review

1. Would you agree or disagree that the description of Isaac's birth is anticlimactic? Why or why not?
2. Why does God tell Abraham to do what Sarah asks in regard to Hagar and Ishmael?
3. What happens to Hagar and Ishmael in the wilderness?
4. What is unique about Hagar and her experiences with the Lord?
5. Now that Isaac is born, why is Abraham still dwelling in the land of the Philistines instead of the land that is his inherited possession?

Genesis Chapter 22

1   *And it came to pass after these things, that God did tempt Abraham, and said unto him, Abraham: and he said, Behold, here I am.*

2 And he said, Take now thy son, thine only son Isaac, whom thou lovest, and get thee into the land of Moriah; and offer him there for a burnt offering upon one of the mountains which I will tell thee of.

3 And Abraham rose up early in the morning, and saddled his ass, and took two of his young men with him, and Isaac his son, and clave the wood for the burnt offering, and rose up, and went unto the place of which God had told him.

4 Then on the third day Abraham lifted up his eyes, and saw the place afar off.

5 And Abraham said unto his young men, Abide ye here with the ass; and I and the lad will go yonder and worship, and come again to you.

6 And Abraham took the wood of the burnt offering, and laid it upon Isaac his son; and he took the fire in his hand, and a knife; and they went both of them together.

7 And Isaac spake unto Abraham his father, and said, My father: and he said, Here am I, my son. And he said, Behold the fire and the wood: but where is the lamb for a burnt offering?

8 And Abraham said, My son, God will provide himself a lamb for a burnt offering: so they went both of them together.

9 And they came to the place which God had told him of; and Abraham built an altar there, and laid the wood in order, and bound Isaac his son, and laid him on the altar upon the wood.

10 And Abraham stretched forth his hand, and took the knife to slay his son.

11 And the angel of the LORD called unto him out of heaven, and said, Abraham, Abraham: and he said, Here am I.

12 And he said, Lay not thine hand upon the lad, neither do thou any thing unto him: for now I know that thou fearest God, seeing thou hast not withheld thy son, thine only son from me.

13 And Abraham lifted up his eyes, and looked, and behold behind him a ram caught in a thicket by his horns: and Abraham went and took the ram, and offered him up for a burnt offering in the stead of his son.

14 And Abraham called the name of that place Jehovah-jireh: as it is said to this day, In the mount of the LORD it shall be seen.

15 And the angel of the LORD called unto Abraham out of heaven the second time,

16 And said, By myself have I sworn, saith the LORD, for because thou hast done this thing, and hast not withheld thy son, thine only son:

17 That in blessing I will bless thee, and in multiplying I will multiply thy seed as the stars of the heaven, and as the sand which is upon the sea shore; and thy seed shall possess the gate of his enemies;

18 And in thy seed shall all the nations of the earth be blessed; because thou hast obeyed my voice.

19 So Abraham returned unto his young men, and they rose up and went together to Beer-sheba; and Abraham dwelt at Beer-sheba.

20 And it came to pass after these things, that it was told Abraham, saying, Behold, Milcah, she hath also born children unto thy brother Nahor;

21 Huz his firstborn, and Buz his brother, and Kemuel the father of Aram,

22 And Chesed, and Hazo, and Pildash, and Jidlaph, and Bethuel.

23 And Bethuel begat Rebekah: these eight Milcah did bear to Nahor, Abraham's brother.

24 And his concubine, whose name was Reumah, she bare also Tebah, and Gaham, and Thahash, and Maachah.

Summary

vv. 1–2

God tests Abraham. God tells Abraham to take his only son Isaac and go to Moriah and offer him for a burnt offering.

vv. 3–8

Abraham gets up early the next morning and takes two servants, Isaac, and wood for the offering. After three days' journey, he sees his destination. He tells his servants to stay with the donkeys and that he and Isaac are going to go and worship and will return. Abraham takes the wood and puts it on Isaac's back. Abraham takes the other supplies, and they continue together. Isaac then asks where the lamb for the offering is, and Abraham replies by stating that God will provide the lamb.

vv. 9–14

They arrive at the place for the offering. Abraham places Isaac on the altar and lifts up his arm with the knife to kill Isaac. Right at that moment, the angel of the Lord speaks to Abraham and tells him not to kill Isaac. Now God knows that Abraham fears Him because he is willing to sacrifice Isaac. Abraham looks and sees a ram in the thicket and offers the ram up as the sacrifice instead of Isaac. Abraham names the place *Jehovah-jireh*, which means "the Lord will provide."[57]

vv. 15–19

The angel of the Lord speaks to Abraham for a second time in this passage. He states that because Abraham is willing to sacrifice Isaac, Abraham will be blessed. The angel repeats that Abraham will be blessed, and God will multiply Abraham's descendants. They will be as many as the stars in the sky and sand on the seashore. Through Abraham, all nations of the earth will be blessed because he obeyed the voice of God. Abraham, Isaac, and the two servants go back to Beer-sheba.

vv. 20–24

Abraham is informed of the birth of his brother Nahor's children, and they are listed.

Commentary

This event has traditionally been described as a test of Abraham's faith. Genesis 22:1 begins with the comment that God is going to test Abraham. The reader is aware that the events that will follow will be a test for Abraham, but Abraham is not aware of this fact.

In verse 2, God requests of Abraham, "Take now thy son, thine only son Isaac, whom thou lovest." Why does God describe Isaac as Abraham's only son when it is common knowledge that Isaac is not Abraham's only son? The Bible clearly

---

[57] The Holy Bible, King James Version (Grand Rapids: Zondervan, 2010).

records that Ishmael is Abraham's firstborn, and we learn after Sarah's death that Abraham remarries and has more sons. By describing Isaac as Abraham's only son, the Bible clarifies that Isaac is going to be the son through whom God's promises will be fulfilled.

In verses 9–10, Abraham builds the altar and actually ties Isaac to it and raises his hand with the knife to kill Isaac. This graphic image of Abraham drawing the knife to kill Isaac is meant to draw the reader into the intensity of the narrative and emphasizes the faith of Abraham. It is right at this moment that the angel of the Lord appears and tells Abraham not to kill Isaac. At this point, Abraham is praised for his obedience, and the angel emphasizes the importance and love Abraham has for Isaac by stating he is Abraham's only son.

In verse 14, Abraham names this area *Jehovah-jireh* meaning "God the provider" or "the Lord will provide." Popular thought has always interpreted this naming to be symbolic of God providing the ram as the substitute for the offering of Isaac. In Abraham's obedience to God, he still understands that God is a provider.

Verses 15–19 reemphasize the renewal of the covenant promises because Abraham has passed the test. These verses are significant because they give an explanation for the test. In verse 16, it states, "because thou hast done this thing, and hast not withheld thy son, thine only son." God says that because Abraham has passed the test, he will be blessed, and God restates many of his early promises to Abraham. Verse 18 reads, "And in thy seed shall all the nations of the earth be blessed; because thou hast obeyed my voice." Abraham's act of faith and obedience in this situation is not only going to be a blessing to his family but also to all humanity.

The request for Isaac's sacrifice may seem strange and even cruel to the modern Christian reader. But this happens toward the end of the Abraham narrative after he experiences the fulfillment of many of God's promises, and he has grown and matured in faith. Although it may seem to require a significant amount of faith for the average Christian, Abraham's faith has been growing for years. I think this passage is an example of the kind of faith that Christians should be striving to achieve, but just as in Abraham's example, it may take a lifetime to accomplish.

The last verses of this chapter list the names of Abraham's brother Nahor's children. Rebekah is listed, and she is connected to the next part of Genesis.

Review

1. Does God tempt Abraham? Does God tempt people at all? (James 1:13–14)
2. What does God ask Abraham to do?
3. Why does God describe Isaac as Abraham's only son?
4. Discuss the significance of Genesis 22:14–18.
5. What connection is there between the presentation of Nahor's children and Isaac?

Genesis Chapter 23

1 *And Sarah was an hundred and seven and twenty years old: these were the years of the life of Sarah.*

2 And Sarah died in Kirjath-arba; the same is Hebron in the land of Canaan: and Abraham came to mourn for Sarah, and to weep for her.

3 And Abraham stood up from before his dead, and spake unto the sons of Heth, saying,

4 I am a stranger and a sojourner with you: give me a possession of a buryingplace with you, that I may bury my dead out of my sight.

5 And the children of Heth answered Abraham, saying unto him,

6 Hear us, my lord: thou art a mighty prince among us: in the choice of our sepulchres bury thy dead; none of us shall withhold from thee his sepulchre, but that thou mayest bury thy dead.

7 And Abraham stood up, and bowed himself to the people of the land, even to the children of Heth.

8 And he communed with them, saying, If it be your mind that I should bury my dead out of my sight; hear me, and intreat for me to Ephron the son of Zohar,

9 That he may give me the cave of Machpelah, which he hath, which is in the end of his field; for as much money as it is worth he shall give it me for a possession of a buryingplace amongst you.

10 And Ephron dwelt among the children of Heth: and Ephron the Hittite answered Abraham in the audience of the children of Heth, even of all that went in at the gate of his city, saying,

11 Nay, my lord, hear me: the field give I thee, and the cave that is therein, I give it thee; in the presence of the sons of my people give I it thee: bury thy dead.

12 And Abraham bowed down himself before the people of the land.

13 And he spake unto Ephron in the audience of the people of the land, saying, But if thou wilt give it, I pray thee, hear me: I will give thee money for the field; take it of me, and I will bury my dead there.

14 And Ephron answered Abraham, saying unto him,

15 My lord, hearken unto me: the land is worth four hundred shekels of silver; what is that betwixt me and thee? bury therefore thy dead.

16 And Abraham hearkened unto Ephron; and Abraham weighed to Ephron the silver, which he had named in the audience of the sons of Heth, four hundred shekels of silver, current money with the merchant.

17 And the field of Ephron, which was in Machpelah, which was before Mamre, the field, and the cave which was therein, and all the trees that were in the field, that were in all the borders round about, were made sure

18 Unto Abraham for a possession in the presence of the children of Heth, before all that went in at the gate of his city.

19 And after this, Abraham buried Sarah his wife in the cave of the field of Machpelah before Mamre: the same is Hebron in the land of Canaan.

20 And the field, and the cave that is therein, were made sure unto Abraham for a possession of a buryingplace by the sons of Heth.

Summary

vv. 1–2

Sarah dies at 127 years old in the land of Canaan, and Abraham grieves her death.

vv. 3–6

Abraham speaks to the sons of Heth and asks them for land to bury Sarah. They respond by saying that Abraham is a prince in the land, and they will give him land to bury Sarah.

vv. 7–12

Abraham asks for the cave at Machpelah that is owned by Ephron son of Soar. Ephron responds by saying he will give Abraham the field.

vv. 13–16

Abraham says he will pay for it. Ephron states the cost is four hundred shekels of silver. Abraham pays Ephron the four hundred shekels of silver.

vv. 17–20

The cave of Machpelah in the land of Canaan is bought by Abraham, and he buries Sarah there.

Commentary

Although God has promised Abraham this land, this will not be fulfilled in Abraham's lifetime. Because Abraham is still a stranger in this land, he has to buy land for burial. He buys a cave and the surrounding land for this purpose. "The sons of Heth" initially are willing to allow Abraham to bury Sarah without charging him, but Abraham offers to pay full price for the land. Abraham's motivation to pay full price is twofold. The first reason is so the people in the land cannot take the land back, and the second reason is to further express that it is God who gives him wealth, not man who gives him any favors or gifts.

Review
1. What happens to Sarah at the beginning of this chapter?
2. What arrangements must Abraham make because of this event?
3. Describe the interaction between Abraham and the sons of Heth.
4. This is the second time we see that Abraham will not take charity from the people in this land. Why does Abraham reject their offer?
5. Who else ends up being buried in this cave?

Genesis Chapter 24

1   *And Abraham was old, and well stricken in age: and the LORD had blessed Abraham in all things.*

2 And Abraham said unto his eldest servant of his house, that ruled over all that he had, Put, I pray thee, thy hand under my thigh:

3 And I will make thee swear by the LORD, the God of heaven, and the God of the earth, that thou shalt not take a wife unto my son of the daughters of the Canaanites, among whom I dwell:

4 But thou shalt go unto my country, and to my kindred, and take a wife unto my son Isaac.

5 And the servant said unto him, Peradventure the woman will not be willing to follow me unto this land: must I needs bring thy son again unto the land from whence thou camest?

6 And Abraham said unto him, Beware thou that thou bring not my son thither again.

7 The LORD God of heaven, which took me from my father's house, and from the land of my kindred, and which spake unto me, and that sware unto me, saying, Unto thy seed will I give this land; he shall send his angel before thee, and thou shalt take a wife unto my son from thence.

8 And if the woman will not be willing to follow thee, then thou shalt be clear from this my oath: only bring not my son thither again.

9 And the servant put his hand under the thigh of Abraham his master, and sware to him concerning that matter.

10 And the servant took ten camels of the camels of his master, and departed; for all the goods of his master were in his hand: and he arose, and went to Mesopotamia, unto the city of Nahor.

11 And he made his camels to kneel down without the city by a well of water at the time of the evening, even the time that women go out to draw water.

12 And he said, O LORD God of my master Abraham, I pray thee, send me good speed this day, and shew kindness unto my master Abraham.

13 Behold, I stand here by the well of water; and the daughters of the men of the city come out to draw water:

14 And let it come to pass, that the damsel to whom I shall say, Let down thy pitcher, I pray thee, that I may drink; and she shall say, Drink, and I will give thy camels drink also: let the same be she that thou hast appointed for thy servant Isaac; and thereby shall I know that thou hast shewed kindness unto my master.

15 And it came to pass, before he had done speaking, that, behold, Rebekah came out, who was born to Bethuel, son of Milcah, the wife of Nahor, Abraham's brother, with her pitcher upon her shoulder.

16 And the damsel was very fair to look upon, a virgin, neither had any man known her: and she went down to the well, and filled her pitcher, and came up.

17 And the servant ran to meet her, and said, Let me, I pray thee, drink a little water of thy pitcher.

18 And she said, Drink, my lord: and she hasted, and let down her pitcher upon her hand, and gave him drink.

19 And when she had done giving him drink, she said, I will draw water for thy camels also, until they have done drinking.

20 And she hasted, and emptied her pitcher into the trough, and ran again unto the well to draw water, and drew for all his camels.

21 And the man wondering at her held his peace, to wit whether the LORD had made his journey prosperous or not.

22 And it came to pass, as the camels had done drinking, that the man took a golden earring of half a shekel weight, and two bracelets for her hands of ten shekels weight of gold;

23 And said, Whose daughter art thou? tell me, I pray thee: is there room in thy father's house for us to lodge in?

24 And she said unto him, I am the daughter of Bethuel the son of Milcah, which she bare unto Nahor.

25 She said moreover unto him, We have both straw and provender enough, and room to lodge in.

26 And the man bowed down his head, and worshipped the LORD.

27 And he said, Blessed be the LORD God of my master Abraham, who hath not left destitute my master of his mercy and his truth: I being in the way, the LORD led me to the house of my master's brethren.

28 And the damsel ran, and told them of her mother's house these things.

29 And Rebekah had a brother, and his name was Laban: and Laban ran out unto the man, unto the well.

30 And it came to pass, when he saw the earring and bracelets upon his sister's hands, and when he heard the words of Rebekah his sister, saying, Thus spake the man unto me; that he came unto the man; and, behold, he stood by the camels at the well.

31 And he said, Come in, thou blessed of the LORD; wherefore standest thou without? for I have prepared the house, and room for the camels.

32 And the man came into the house: and he ungirded his camels, and gave straw and provender for the camels, and water to wash his feet, and the men's feet that were with him.

33 And there was set meat before him to eat: but he said, I will not eat, until I have told mine errand. And he said, Speak on.

34 And he said, I am Abraham's servant.

35 And the LORD hath blessed my master greatly; and he is become great: and he hath given him flocks, and herds, and silver, and gold, and menservants, and maidservants, and camels, and asses.

36 And Sarah my master's wife bare a son to my master when she was old: and unto him hath he given all that he hath.

37 And my master made me swear, saying, Thou shalt not take a wife to my son of the daughters of the Canaanites, in whose land I dwell:

38 But thou shalt go unto my father's house, and to my kindred, and take a wife unto my son.

39 And I said unto my master, Peradventure the woman will not follow me.

40 And he said unto me, The LORD, before whom I walk, will send his angel with thee, and prosper thy way; and thou shalt take a wife for my son of my kindred, and of my father's house:

41 Then shalt thou be clear from this my oath, when thou comest to my kindred; and if they give not thee one, thou shalt be clear from my oath.

42 And I came this day unto the well, and said, O LORD God of my master Abraham, if now thou do prosper my way which I go:

43 Behold, I stand by the well of water; and it shall come to pass, that when the virgin cometh forth to draw water, and I say to her, Give me, I pray thee, a little water of thy pitcher to drink;

44 And she say to me, Both drink thou, and I will also draw for thy camels: let the same be the woman whom the LORD hath appointed out for my master's son.

45 And before I had done speaking in mine heart, behold, Rebekah came forth with her pitcher on her shoulder; and she went down unto the well, and drew water: and I said unto her, Let me drink, I pray thee.

46 And she made haste, and let down her pitcher from her shoulder, and said, Drink, and I will give thy camels drink also: so I drank, and she made the camels drink also.

47 And I asked her, and said, Whose daughter art thou? And she said, The daughter of Bethuel, Nahor's son, whom Milcah bare unto him: and I put the earring upon her face, and the bracelets upon her hands.

48 And I bowed down my head, and worshipped the LORD, and blessed the LORD God of my master Abraham, which had led me in the right way to take my master's brother's daughter unto his son.

49 And now if ye will deal kindly and truly with my master, tell me: and if not, tell me; that I may turn to the right hand, or to the left.

50 Then Laban and Bethuel answered and said, The thing proceedeth from the LORD: we cannot speak unto thee bad or good.

51 Behold, Rebekah is before thee, take her, and go, and let her be thy master's son's wife, as the LORD hath spoken.

52 And it came to pass, that, when Abraham's servant heard their words, he worshipped the LORD, bowing himself to the earth.

53 And the servant brought forth jewels of silver, and jewels of gold, and raiment, and gave them to Rebekah: he gave also to her brother and to her mother precious things.

54 And they did eat and drink, he and the men that were with him, and tarried all night; and they rose up in the morning, and he said, Send me away unto my master.

55 And her brother and her mother said, Let the damsel abide with us a few days, at the least ten; after that she shall go.

56 And he said unto them, Hinder me not, seeing the LORD hath prospered my way; send me away that I may go to my master.

57 And they said, We will call the damsel, and enquire at her mouth.

58 And they called Rebekah, and said unto her, Wilt thou go with this man? And she said, I will go.

59 And they sent away Rebekah their sister, and her nurse, and Abraham's servant, and his men.

60 And they blessed Rebekah, and said unto her, Thou art our sister, be thou the mother of thousands of millions, and let thy seed possess the gate of those which hate them.

61 And Rebekah arose, and her damsels, and they rode upon the camels, and followed the man: and the servant took Rebekah, and went his way.

62 And Isaac came from the way of the well Lahai-roi; for he dwelt in the south country.

63 And Isaac went out to meditate in the field at the eventide: and he lifted up his eyes, and saw, and, behold, the camels were coming.

64 And Rebekah lifted up her eyes, and when she saw Isaac, she lighted off the camel.

65 For she had said unto the servant, What man is this that walketh in the field to meet us? And the servant had said, It is my master: therefore she took a vail, and covered herself.

66 And the servant told Isaac all things that he had done.

67 And Isaac brought her into his mother Sarah's tent, and took Rebekah, and she became his wife; and he loved her: and Isaac was comforted after his mother's death.

Summary

vv. 1–4

Abraham is old, and God has blessed him. Abraham asks his eldest servant to put his hand under his thigh and make a vow that he will not allow Isaac to marry a Canaanite woman. Then he asks his servant to go to Abraham's old country and to his family to get a wife for Isaac.

vv. 5–9

His servant asks what to do if the woman is unwilling to come. Shouldn't he bring Isaac? Abraham says that God will send an angel before the servant and not to take Isaac. If the woman is not willing to come back with the servant, then Abraham will not hold him to this promise. The servant places his hand underneath Abraham's thigh and swears to do this.

vv. 10–14

The servant brings "many" goods for the potential bride and travels to Mesopotamia in the city of Nahor. The servant prays that God will give him success. As the servant stands by the city well, he prays that the woman who offers him a drink of water and water for his camels from the well will be Isaac's bride.

vv. 15–16

Before he finishes praying, Rebekah comes to the well. She is the daughter of
Bethuel. He is the son of Nahor, who is Abraham's brother, and his wife Milcah.
Rebekah is a virgin.

vv. 17–20

Rebekah gives the servant water to drink and waters his camels also.

vv. 21–27

After he and the camels are finished drinking, the servant asks Rebekah who
she is. She replies by saying that she is the daughter of Bethuel, who is the son of
Milcah and Nahor. She also states that they have a place for him to stay, and he
praises God for leading him to Abraham's family.

vv. 28–33

Rebekah tells her family what has happened. Her brother Laban meets
Abraham's servant and invites him to their house. The servant comes into the
house and washes his feet. They prepare food for him to eat, but he will not eat
until he tells them why he came.

vv. 34–49

The servant states that he is Abraham's servant and that Sarah has had a son
and that Abraham has given that son all he has. He relates how Abraham made
him swear that he will not allow Isaac to marry a Canaanite woman and told him
to go to Abraham's family's country to find a wife and that God has sent an angel
before him. If the woman will not go with the servant, then Abraham will not hold
him to the promise. The servant describes how he met Rebekah at the well and
asks if Rebekah's answer is yes or no.

vv. 50–59

Rebekah decides to become Isaac's wife. The servant gives Rebekah and her
family gifts. They all eat. The servant wakes up the next morning and is ready to
leave. Her family wants her to stay for at least ten days. But the servant responds
that he does not want to delay going back since his trip has been successful.
Rebekah's mother and brother say they will let her decide. She decides that she
will leave, so she leaves with the servant and her nurse.

vv. 60–67

They bless Rebekah and say she will be the mother of thousands of millions.
She returns with Abraham's servant. Isaac is in the field, and Rebekah sees him

and asks the servant who he is. The servant replies that it is Isaac, and she covers herself with her veil. The servant tells Isaac everything that has happened. Isaac takes Rebekah into his tent and makes her his wife.

Commentary

This is the longest chapter in Genesis. Many of the events are repeated because the characters need to be informed of the events even though the reader is aware of what has happened.

Abraham asks his servant to go back to his old country to find a wife for Isaac. Abraham asks his servant to put his hand under his thigh, which is a sign of an oath.[58] There are two things that Abraham makes clear to his servant. He does not want Isaac to marry a Canaanite, and he does not want Isaac to go back to the land of his family. The land of Canaan is the land God has promised Abraham's descendants, so Isaac should stay in the land that God has promised. Also, the Canaanites are not a "blessed" people because God is going to remove them from the land in order to give it to Abraham's descendants.

There is a theme throughout the Bible of God's chosen people not intermarrying with those who do not believe in God. All throughout the Old Testament, God makes it clear that He does not want His people to intermarry with unbelievers. Some Christians have taken this out of context and interpreted it to mean not marrying someone of a different race or ethnicity, but what God is concerned about is spiritual and religious differences, not ethnic ones. He does not want His chosen people's hearts to be turned away from Him by marrying people who do not believe in God.

Now that Isaac is married, he and Rebekah become heirs to the promise and blessings of God. Essentially, Isaac replaces Abraham, and Rebekah replaces Sarah. Her family even gives Rebekah a similar blessing to what God stated to Sarah by saying she will be the mother to thousands of millions.

Review
1. Why doesn't Abraham want Isaac to marry a Canaanite woman?
2. What is Abraham's servant's prayer in regard to finding Isaac's wife?
3. How are Abraham and Isaac related to Nahor, Laban, and Rebekah?
4. How is Rebekah's blessing in Genesis 24:60 similar to Sarah's blessing in Genesis 17:16?
5. Why is this chapter so long?

---

[58] Wenham, *Word Biblical Commentary*, 2:145.

Genesis Chapter 25

1 *Then again Abraham took a wife, and her name was Keturah.*
2 And she bare him Zimran, and Jokshan, and Medan, and Midian, and Ishbak, and Shuah.

3 And Jokshan begat Sheba, and Dedan. And the sons of Dedan were Asshurim, and Letushim, and Leummim.

4 And the sons of Midian; Ephah, and Epher, and Hanoch, and Abida, and Eldaah. All these were the children of Keturah.

5 And Abraham gave all that he had unto Isaac.

6 But unto the sons of the concubines, which Abraham had, Abraham gave gifts, and sent them away from Isaac his son, while he yet lived, eastward, unto the east country.

7 And these are the days of the years of Abraham's life which he lived, an hundred threescore and fifteen years.

8 Then Abraham gave up the ghost, and died in a good old age, an old man, and full of years; and was gathered to his people.

9 And his sons Isaac and Ishmael buried him in the cave of Machpelah, in the field of Ephron the son of Zohar the Hittite, which is before Mamre;

10 The field which Abraham purchased of the sons of Heth: there was Abraham buried, and Sarah his wife.

11 And it came to pass after the death of Abraham, that God blessed his son Isaac; and Isaac dwelt by the well Lahai-roi.

12 Now these are the generations of Ishmael, Abraham's son, whom Hagar the Egyptian, Sarah's handmaid, bare unto Abraham:

13 And these are the names of the sons of Ishmael, by their names, according to their generations: the firstborn of Ishmael, Nebajoth; and Kedar, and Adbeel, and Mibsam,

14 And Mishma, and Dumah, and Massa,

15 Hadar, and Tema, Jetur, Naphish, and Kedemah:

16 These are the sons of Ishmael, and these are their names, by their towns, and by their castles; twelve princes according to their nations.

17 And these are the years of the life of Ishmael, an hundred and thirty and seven years: and he gave up the ghost and died; and was gathered unto his people.

18 And they dwelt from Havilah unto Shur, that is before Egypt, as thou goest toward Assyria: and he died in the presence of all his brethren.

19 And these are the generations of Isaac, Abraham's son: Abraham begat Isaac:

20 And Isaac was forty years old when he took Rebekah to wife, the daughter of Bethuel the Syrian of Padan-aram, the sister to Laban the Syrian.

21 And Isaac intreated the LORD for his wife, because she was barren: and the LORD was entreated of him, and Rebekah his wife conceived.

22 And the children struggled together within her; and she said, If it be so, why am I thus? And she went to enquire of the LORD.

23 And the LORD said unto her, Two nations are in thy womb, and two manner of people shall be separated from thy bowels; and the one people shall be stronger than the other people; and the elder shall serve the younger.

24 And when her days to be delivered were fulfilled, behold, there were twins in her womb.

25 And the first came out red, all over like an hairy garment; and they called his name Esau.

26 And after that came his brother out, and his hand took hold on Esau's heel; and his name was called Jacob: and Isaac was threescore years old when she bare them.

27 And the boys grew: and Esau was a cunning hunter, a man of the field; and Jacob was a plain man, dwelling in tents.

28 And Isaac loved Esau, because he did eat of his venison: but Rebekah loved Jacob.

29 And Jacob sod pottage: and Esau came from the field, and he was faint:

30 And Esau said to Jacob, Feed me, I pray thee, with that same red pottage; for I am faint: therefore was his name called Edom.

31 And Jacob said, Sell me this day thy birthright.

32 And Esau said, Behold, I am at the point to die: and what profit shall this birthright do to me?

33 And Jacob said, Swear to me this day; and he sware unto him: and he sold his birthright unto Jacob.

34 Then Jacob gave Esau bread and pottage of lentiles; and he did eat and drink, and rose up, and went his way: thus Esau despised his birthright.

Summary

vv. 1–6

Abraham remarries a woman named Keturah. She has six children with Abraham. Abraham gives his inheritance to Isaac and gifts to his other children and sends them to a land in the East away from Isaac.

vv. 7–11

Abraham dies at 175 years old. Isaac and Ishmael come and bury him in the cave of Machpelah with Sarah, which Abraham bought from Ephron the Hittite. After Abraham's death, God blesses Isaac.

vv. 12–18

Moses lists Ishmael's twelve sons. Each son becomes a prince of a nation. Ishmael dies at 137 years old surrounded by his family.

vv. 19–26

Now this begins the story of Isaac and his descendants. Isaac is forty years old when he marries Rebekah. Isaac prays for Rebekah because she is barren, and she conceives. The children struggle in her womb, and she asks the Lord about it. He states there are two children representing two nations. One will be stronger than the other. The older will serve the younger. Rebekah delivers twins. The older one is *Esau*, which means "red and hairy," and the younger one is *Jacob*, which means "deceiver."[59]

vv. 27–34

Esau becomes a hunter, while Jacob dwells in tents. Isaac favors Esau because Isaac enjoys eating Esau's venison, but Rebekah favors Jacob. Jacob is cooking pottage, and Esau comes from the field tired and faint. Esau asks Jacob for some pottage. Jacob responds by asking Esau to sell his birthright. Esau states that he is close to death, so what is the point of the birthright if he dies? Esau swears to

---

[59] Douglas Mangum, "Jacob, Son of Isaac," in *The Lexham Bible Dictionary*, eds. John D. Barry et al.

Jacob his birthright. Jacob gives Esau the pottage. Esau does not value his birthright.

Commentary

Although Abraham remarries and has other children, he gives his wealth to Isaac because Isaac is the covenant offspring. One child to note who is born from Abraham's wife Keturah is Midian because he becomes the father of the Midianites, who the Israelites interact with throughout the Old Testament.

Abraham dies at 175 years old. Isaac and Ishmael bury him in the same cave as Sarah. The writer only mentions Isaac and Ishmael because they are the sons of Abraham who are the most significant. Ishmael is the firstborn, and Isaac is the son of promise and blessings. Ishmael and his descendants are still blessed because of Abraham, just as God has promised. Ishmael has twelve sons who become leaders of twelve nations, which is similar to the twelve sons of Jacob who become the twelve tribes of Israel.

Rebekah is also barren, like Sarah, and God miraculously makes Rebekah conceive. This is another example that it is God who blesses. The covenant with Abraham that God will multiply his descendants is emphasized because the text makes it clear that God causes her to conceive.

This passage ends with Jacob "buying" Esau's birthright. The birthright has a significant meaning. The birthright is a special blessing for the eldest son. It also includes a significant portion of the inheritance because the eldest son is required to take care of his mother and any unwed sisters. When the father dies, it is the eldest son who becomes the man of the house, so he is given great respect.

Later, during the time of Moses, the birthright also included that the oldest would be the priest of the home, receive a double portion of material wealth, and succeed in the official authority of the father. In Exodus 22:29 and Deuteronomy 21:15–17, these verses describe how the firstborn is the first fruit of his father's strength.

Because Esau sells his birthright for pottage, it appears that he does not value his birthright. In contrast, Jacob seems to understand and value the significance of the birthright. Although we may want to feel sorry for Esau because he is faint, and we may feel that Jacob takes advantage of Esau and tricks him into giving up his birthright, that is not the case. Although Jacob could share the food with Esau, Esau is not tricked into giving up his birthright. He sells it willingly.

Review

1. Although Abraham remarries and has other children, why does he leave his inheritance to Isaac?
2. How old is Abraham when he dies, and where is he buried?
3. What is significant about both Sarah and Rebekah not being able to conceive?
4. What prophecy does God give Rebekah in regard to her children?
5. What is meant by "Esau despised his birthright" in Genesis 25:34?

Genesis Chapter 26

1 And there was a famine in the land, beside the first famine that was in the days of Abraham. And Isaac went unto Abimelech king of the Philistines unto Gerar.

2 And the LORD appeared unto him, and said, Go not down into Egypt; dwell in the land which I shall tell thee of:

3 Sojourn in this land, and I will be with thee, and will bless thee; for unto thee, and unto thy seed, I will give all these countries, and I will perform the oath which I sware unto Abraham thy father;

4 And I will make thy seed to multiply as the stars of heaven, and will give unto thy seed all these countries; and in thy seed shall all the nations of the earth be blessed;

5 Because that Abraham obeyed my voice, and kept my charge, my commandments, my statutes, and my laws.

6 And Isaac dwelt in Gerar:

7 And the men of the place asked him of his wife; and he said, She is my sister: for he feared to say, She is my wife; lest, said he, the men of the place should kill me for Rebekah; because she was fair to look upon.

8 And it came to pass, when he had been there a long time, that Abimelech king of the Philistines looked out at a window, and saw, and, behold, Isaac was sporting with Rebekah his wife.

9 And Abimelech called Isaac, and said, Behold, of a surety she is thy wife: and how saidst thou, She is my sister? And Isaac said unto him, Because I said, Lest I die for her.

10 And Abimelech said, What is this thou hast done unto us? one of the people might lightly have lien with thy wife, and thou shouldest have brought guiltiness upon us.

11 And Abimelech charged all his people, saying, He that toucheth this man or his wife shall surely be put to death.

12 Then Isaac sowed in that land, and received in the same year an hundredfold: and the LORD blessed him.

13 And the man waxed great, and went forward, and grew until he became very great:

14 For he had possession of flocks, and possession of herds, and great store of servants: and the Philistines envied him.

15 For all the wells which his father's servants had digged in the days of Abraham his father, the Philistines had stopped them, and filled them with earth.

16 And Abimelech said unto Isaac, Go from us; for thou art much mightier than we.

17 And Isaac departed thence, and pitched his tent in the valley of Gerar, and dwelt there.

18 And Isaac digged again the wells of water, which they had digged in the days of Abraham his father; for the Philistines had stopped them after the death of Abraham: and he called their names after the names by which his father had called them.

19 And Isaac's servants digged in the valley, and found there a well of springing water.

20 And the herdmen of Gerar did strive with Isaac's herdmen, saying, The water is ours: and he called the name of the well Esek; because they strove with him.

21 And they digged another well, and strove for that also: and he called the name of it Sitnah.

22 And he removed from thence, and digged another well; and for that they strove not: and he called the name of it Rehoboth; and he said, For now the LORD hath made room for us, and we shall be fruitful in the land.

23 And he went up from thence to Beer-sheba.

24 And the LORD appeared unto him the same night, and said, I am the God of Abraham thy father: fear not, for I am with thee, and will bless thee, and multiply thy seed for my servant Abraham's sake.

25 And he builded an altar there, and called upon the name of the LORD, and pitched his tent there: and there Isaac's servants digged a well.

26 Then Abimelech went to him from Gerar, and Ahuzzath one of his friends, and Phichol the chief captain of his army.

27 And Isaac said unto them, Wherefore come ye to me, seeing ye hate me, and have sent me away from you?

28 And they said, We saw certainly that the LORD was with thee: and we said, Let there be now an oath betwixt us, even betwixt us and thee, and let us make a covenant with thee;

29 That thou wilt do us no hurt, as we have not touched thee, and as we have done unto thee nothing but good, and have sent thee away in peace: thou art now the blessed of the LORD.

30 And he made them a feast, and they did eat and drink.

31 And they rose up betimes in the morning, and sware one to another: and Isaac sent them away, and they departed from him in peace.

32 And it came to pass the same day, that Isaac's servants came, and told him concerning the well which they had digged, and said unto him, We have found water.

33 And he called it Shebah: therefore the name of the city is Beer-sheba unto this day.

34 And Esau was forty years old when he took to wife Judith the daughter of Beeri the Hittite, and Bashemath the daughter of Elon the Hittite:

35 Which were a grief of mind unto Isaac and to Rebekah.

Summary

vv. 1–5

There is a famine in the land, and Isaac travels to Gerar, the land of Abimelech, king of the Philistines. Isaac is planning to go to Egypt, but God tells him to stay in Gerar. God promises Isaac blessings if he is obedient: "I will give thee countries ... I will make thy seed to multiply as the stars of the heaven ... and in thy seed all the nations of the earth be blessed."

vv. 6–7

When they are in Gerar, Isaac states that Rebekah is his sister. He is afraid that they will kill him and take Rebekah because she is beautiful.

vv. 8–11

Abimelech sees Isaac caressing Rebekah. He confronts Isaac and says he knows Rebekah is Isaac's wife. Abimelech asks why Isaac said she is his sister. Isaac replies that he was afraid he would be killed. Abimelech says that someone could have had sex with her and brought guilt on himself. Then Abimelech tells his people not to touch Isaac or his wife, or they will be put to death.

vv. 12–16

Isaac sows in the land and receives a hundredfold blessing. The wells that Abraham's servants dug, the Philistines have filled with dirt. Abimelech tells Isaac to leave because he has become so wealthy that he has become mightier than the Philistines.

vv. 17–22

Isaac leaves the land, but his servants dig up the wells that Abraham's servants dug. The wells are given the same name that Abraham had given them, and they flow with water again. The herdsman of Gerar and Isaac's herdsmen argue over the wells. Isaac moves from that area and builds another well, and there is no argument among the herdsmen. God blesses Isaac in that area.

vv. 23–25

Isaac goes to Beer-sheba. The Lord appears to Isaac and identifies Himself as the God of Abraham and says that He is with Isaac and will multiply his seed for Abraham's sake. Isaac builds an altar and digs a well there.

vv. 26–33

Abimelech comes to Isaac with Ahuzzath and Phichol, the captain of Abimelech's army, to obtain a peace agreement with him. Isaac asks why Abimelech has come to him when Abimelech must not have liked him to send him away. Abimelech explains that he sees that God is with Isaac and would like to make a covenant with Isaac. Isaac makes them a feast and makes a covenant, and they depart in peace. The next day, his servants tell him there is now water in the well they have just dug. Beer-Sheba means "well of seven" or "oath," so Isaac makes an oath with Abimelech, and God blesses Isaac.

vv. 34–35

Esau marries two Hittite women, which his parents disapprove of.

Commentary

Just as in Abraham's time, there is a famine, and Isaac begins to travel toward Egypt, but Isaac stops in Gerar. This time God tells Isaac to stay in Gerar, and He will bless Isaac there.

In the same fashion as his father, Isaac lies to Abimelech about his wife and states that she is his sister. The similarities continue because Abimelech discovers the lie and confronts Isaac. Although we do not know why Abraham and Isaac both lie instead of trusting God, what we can learn from these three situations is that killing a man to take his wife, especially if she is beautiful, must have been a common and well-known practice at the time, and they were both afraid of death. Despite their behavior in these situations, God still upholds the covenant and blesses them. Although Abimelech was deceived, he still protects Isaac and Rebekah by commanding that no one touch them.

Although there is a famine in the land, Isaac is obedient and stays in Gerar. God blesses Isaac, and he gains wealth. Now that Abraham is dead, the covenant that God had with Abraham belongs to Isaac. Although Abraham does not live to see the totality of God's covenant fulfilled, it is important to understand that the promises of God still stand. God restates the promises of multiplying his seed and obtaining land for Isaac's descendants. God will fulfill His promise to Isaac and his descendants because Abraham was obedient and kept God's commandments.

Esau marries two women whom his parents do not approve of because they are Hittites. Isaac and Rebekah do not approve of Esau's wives for the same reason that Abraham did not want Isaac to marry a Canaanite woman, which is that they served pagan gods. This is just another example that God does not want Abraham's descendants to intermarry with nations that believe in false gods. God knows that this will turn His people away from Him, and this is what happens many times in the Israelites' history.

Review
1. Compare and contrast Genesis 26:1–7 with Genesis 12:14–20 and Genesis 20.
2. How does Abimelech discover he is being deceived by Isaac and Rebekah?
3. Why is Isaac able to prosper during the famine?
4. What is significant about Beer-Sheba and the blessing God gives to Isaac there?
5. Why is it a grief to Isaac and Rebekah that Esau marries two Hittite women?

Genesis Chapter 27

1   *And it came to pass, that when Isaac was old, and his eyes were dim, so that he could not see, he called Esau his eldest son, and said unto him, My son: and he said unto him, Behold, here am I.*

2 And he said, Behold now, I am old, I know not the day of my death:

3 Now therefore take, I pray thee, thy weapons, thy quiver and thy bow, and go out to the field, and take me some venison;

4 And make me savoury meat, such as I love, and bring it to me, that I may eat; that my soul may bless thee before I die.

5 And Rebekah heard when Isaac spake to Esau his son. And Esau went to the field to hunt for venison, and to bring it.

6 And Rebekah spake unto Jacob her son, saying, Behold, I heard thy father speak unto Esau thy brother, saying,

7 Bring me venison, and make me savoury meat, that I may eat, and bless thee before the LORD before my death.

8 Now therefore, my son, obey my voice according to that which I command thee.

9 Go now to the flock, and fetch me from thence two good kids of the goats; and I will make them savoury meat for thy father, such as he loveth:

10 And thou shalt bring it to thy father, that he may eat, and that he may bless thee before his death.

11 And Jacob said to Rebekah his mother, Behold, Esau my brother is a hairy man, and I am a smooth man:

12 My father peradventure will feel me, and I shall seem to him as a deceiver; and I shall bring a curse upon me, and not a blessing.

13 And his mother said unto him, Upon me be thy curse, my son: only obey my voice, and go fetch me them.

14 And he went, and fetched, and brought them to his mother: and his mother made savoury meat, such as his father loved.

15 And Rebekah took goodly raiment of her eldest son Esau, which were with her in the house, and put them upon Jacob her younger son:

16 And she put the skins of the kids of the goats upon his hands, and upon the smooth of his neck:

17 And she gave the savoury meat and the bread, which she had prepared, into the hand of her son Jacob.

18 And he came unto his father, and said, My father: and he said, Here am I; who art thou, my son?

19 And Jacob said unto his father, I am Esau thy firstborn; I have done according as thou badest me: arise, I pray thee, sit and eat of my venison, that thy soul may bless me.

20 And Isaac said unto his son, How is it that thou hast found it so quickly, my son? And he said, Because the LORD thy God brought it to me.

21 And Isaac said unto Jacob, Come near, I pray thee, that I may feel thee, my son, whether thou be my very son Esau or not.

22 And Jacob went near unto Isaac his father; and he felt him, and said, The voice is Jacob's voice, but the hands are the hands of Esau.

23 And he discerned him not, because his hands were hairy, as his brother Esau's hands: so he blessed him.

24 And he said, Art thou my very son Esau? And he said, I am.

25 And he said, Bring it near to me, and I will eat of my son's venison, that my soul may bless thee. And he brought it near to him, and he did eat: and he brought him wine, and he drank.

26 And his father Isaac said unto him, Come near now, and kiss me, my son.

27 And he came near, and kissed him: and he smelled the smell of his raiment, and blessed him, and said, See, the smell of my son is as the smell of a field which the LORD hath blessed:

28 Therefore God give thee of the dew of heaven, and the fatness of the earth, and plenty of corn and wine:

29 Let people serve thee, and nations bow down to thee: be lord over thy brethren, and let thy mother's sons bow down to thee: cursed be every one that curseth thee, and blessed be he that blesseth thee.

30 And it came to pass, as soon as Isaac had made an end of blessing Jacob, and Jacob was yet scarce gone out from the presence of Isaac his father, that Esau his brother came in from his hunting.

31 And he also had made savoury meat, and brought it unto his father, and said unto his father, Let my father arise, and eat of his son's venison, that thy soul may bless me.

32 And Isaac his father said unto him, Who art thou? And he said, I am thy son, thy firstborn Esau.

33 And Isaac trembled very exceedingly, and said, Who? where is he that hath taken venison, and brought it me, and I have eaten of all before thou camest, and have blessed him? yea, and he shall be blessed.

34 And when Esau heard the words of his father, he cried with a great and exceeding bitter cry, and said unto his father, Bless me, even me also, O my father.

35 And he said, Thy brother came with subtilty, and hath taken away thy blessing.

36 And he said, Is not he rightly named Jacob? for he hath supplanted me these two times: he took away my birthright; and, behold, now he hath taken away my blessing. And he said, Hast thou not reserved a blessing for me?

37 And Isaac answered and said unto Esau, Behold, I have made him thy lord, and all his brethren have I given to him for servants; and with corn and wine have I sustained him: and what shall I do now unto thee, my son?

38 And Esau said unto his father, Hast thou but one blessing, my father? bless me, even me also, O my father. And Esau lifted up his voice, and wept.

39 And Isaac his father answered and said unto him, Behold, thy dwelling shall be the fatness of the earth, and of the dew of heaven from above;

40 And by thy sword shalt thou live, and shalt serve thy brother; and it shall come to pass when thou shalt have the dominion, that thou shalt break his yoke from off thy neck.

41 And Esau hated Jacob because of the blessing wherewith his father blessed him: and Esau said in his heart, The days of mourning for my father are at hand; then will I slay my brother Jacob.

42 And these words of Esau her elder son were told to Rebekah: and she sent and called Jacob her younger son, and said unto him, Behold, thy brother Esau, as touching thee, doth comfort himself, purposing to kill thee.

43 Now therefore, my son, obey my voice; and arise, flee thou to Laban my brother to Haran;

44 And tarry with him a few days, until thy brother's fury turn away;

45 Until thy brother's anger turn away from thee, and he forget that which thou hast done to him: then I will send, and fetch thee from thence: why should I be deprived also of you both in one day?

46 And Rebekah said to Isaac, I am weary of my life because of the daughters of Heth: if Jacob take a wife of the daughters of Heth, such as these which are of the daughters of the land, what good shall my life do me?

Summary

vv. 1–4

Isaac is old with poor eyesight, and he asks Esau to go hunt game and prepare a meal for him so that he may bless Esau. Esau goes out to do what his father has asked him.

vv. 5–17

Rebekah overhears this conversation. She tells Jacob to get two goats, and she will prepare the meal the way Isaac requested so Jacob can go in to Isaac, and Isaac will bless him instead of Esau. Jacob has some concerns this will not work because Esau is hairy, and Jacob is not. Jacob is afraid that Isaac will discover he is trying to deceive him and curse him instead. So Rebekah puts Esau's coat on Jacob and places animal skins on his arms so he will smell and feel like Esau.

vv. 18–29

Jacob goes to Isaac with the food that Rebekah prepares, and their deception works. Isaac is convinced that Jacob is Esau because he smells and feels like Esau, and Isaac blesses Jacob. Isaac states that Jacob's land will be blessed. He also states that nations will bow down to Jacob and that he will be lord over his brother. Isaac ends by saying that those who curse Jacob will be cursed and those who bless Jacob will be blessed.

vv. 30–40

Almost as soon as Jacob leaves, Esau returns and presents the food he has made for Isaac and states he is ready for his blessing. Isaac reveals to Esau that Jacob deceived him and received Esau's blessing. Esau states that Jacob is correctly named because he has "stolen" Esau's birthright and blessing. Isaac does "bless" Esau. Isaac states that Esau's descendants will eventually establish their own nation.

vv. 41–46

Esau hates Jacob and decides he will wait until after Isaac dies to kill Jacob. Rebekah is told about Esau's plans and tells Jacob that he should go to Haran and stay with her brother Laban until Esau's anger subsides. She concludes by stating to Isaac how she is not happy with the wives Esau has picked, implying that another reason to send Jacob to Haran is that Jacob will get a wife from his own people and please his parents.

Commentary

This chapter focuses on Isaac's blessing. The blessing is of great significance, similar to a swearing-in ceremony. The blessings of the father to the son are sealed and given by God. Once the blessing is given, it cannot be taken back. Rebekah and Jacob work together to deceive Isaac into giving Jacob the blessing. In verse 35, Isaac states that Jacob came with subtlety, which is the same term used in Genesis 3:1 to describe the serpent that deceived Eve. Esau also comments about Jacob's character, saying that he was accurately named *Jacob*, which means "supplanter" or "deceiver," because he has "deceived" Esau out of his blessing.

Isaac repeats many of the blessings that God gave to him and to Abraham when he blesses Jacob. In verse 29 it says, "Cursed be every one that curseth thee, and blessed be he that blesseth thee." This is part of the covenant blessing that God has made with Abraham and continues with his son and now his grandson.

This chapter also demonstrates the issue of sibling rivalry, which is prevalent throughout Genesis. Sibling rivalry is simply siblings competing for the same thing, which is usually their parents' love and attention. This issue actually started with Cain and Abel and has continued with the descendants of Abraham. Although Esau does not get the chance, he hates Jacob and desires to kill him just as Cain hated Abel and killed him. Sibling rivalry is seen in each generation from Abraham to Joseph. Abraham favors Isaac over Ishmael. Isaac favors Esau, but Rebekah favors Jacob. Jacob favors Joseph over his other sons.

Abraham, Isaac, and Jacob are considered patriarchs or the founding fathers of the Jewish and Christian religions.[60] This is essentially the end of Isaac's narrative and the beginning of Jacob's narrative. Although Isaac is considered a patriarch, Isaac's story is substantially shorter than Abraham's and Jacob's and even Joseph's (who is not considered a patriarch). Although the chapters devoted to his life might be short, Isaac is significant. Isaac himself is evidence of a miracle and the fulfillment of a promise from God.

Food for thought: God gives Rebekah a prophecy about Esau and Jacob before they are born, saying that Esau will serve Jacob. Does Rebekah plan this deception (because she knows of the prophecy) so that it will be fulfilled? Does God already know that Rebekah will plan this deception before giving her the prophecy? This question is essentially about the sovereignty of God and the free will of mankind. Although God is sovereign, meaning that He has all authority, He does give man free will, meaning that men can choose their destiny.

---

[60] "Patmos," in *The Lexham Bible Dictionary*, eds. John D. Barry et al.

Review

1. What is important about the blessing given from the father to the oldest son?
2. Discuss the meanings of Esau's and Jacob's names.
3. How do Rebekah and Jacob deceive Isaac?
4. What is Esau's response once he discovers that Jacob has stolen his blessing?
5. Why does Jacob leave to travel to Haran?

Genesis Chapter 28

1 *And Isaac called Jacob, and blessed him, and charged him, and said unto him, Thou shalt not take a wife of the daughters of Canaan.*

2 Arise, go to Padan-aram, to the house of Bethuel thy mother's father; and take thee a wife from thence of the daughters of Laban thy mother's brother.

3 And God Almighty bless thee, and make thee fruitful, and multiply thee, that thou mayest be a multitude of people;

4 And give thee the blessing of Abraham, to thee, and to thy seed with thee; that thou mayest inherit the land wherein thou art a stranger, which God gave unto Abraham.

5 And Isaac sent away Jacob: and he went to Padan-aram unto Laban, son of Bethuel the Syrian, the brother of Rebekah, Jacob's and Esau's mother.

6 When Esau saw that Isaac had blessed Jacob, and sent him away to Padan-aram, to take him a wife from thence; and that as he blessed him he gave him a charge, saying, Thou shalt not take a wife of the daughters of Canaan;

7 And that Jacob obeyed his father and his mother, and was gone to Padan-aram;

8 And Esau seeing that the daughters of Canaan pleased not Isaac his father;

9 Then went Esau unto Ishmael, and took unto the wives which he had Mahalath the daughter of Ishmael Abraham's son, the sister of Nebajoth, to be his wife.

10 And Jacob went out from Beers-heba, and went toward Haran.

11 And he lighted upon a certain place, and tarried there all night, because the sun was set; and he took of the stones of that place, and put them for his pillows, and lay down in that place to sleep.

12 And he dreamed, and behold a ladder set up on the earth, and the top of it reached to heaven: and behold the angels of God ascending and descending on it.

13 And, behold, the LORD stood above it, and said, I am the LORD God of Abraham thy father, and the God of Isaac: the land whereon thou liest, to thee will I give it, and to thy seed;

14 And thy seed shall be as the dust of the earth, and thou shalt spread abroad to the west, and to the east, and to the north, and to the south: and in thee and in thy seed shall all the families of the earth be blessed.

15 And, behold, I am with thee, and will keep thee in all places whither thou goest, and will bring thee again into this land; for I will not leave thee, until I have done that which I have spoken to thee of.

16 And Jacob awaked out of his sleep, and he said, Surely the LORD is in this place; and I knew it not.

17 And he was afraid, and said, How dreadful is this place! this is none other but the house of God, and this is the gate of heaven.

18 And Jacob rose up early in the morning, and took the stone that he had put for his pillows, and set it up for a pillar, and poured oil upon the top of it.

19 And he called the name of that place Beth-el: but the name of that city was called Luz at the first.

20 And Jacob vowed a vow, saying, If God will be with me, and will keep me in this way that I go, and will give me bread to eat, and raiment to put on,

21 So that I come again to my father's house in peace; then shall the LORD be my God:

22 And this stone, which I have set for a pillar, shall be God's house: and of all that thou shalt give me I will surely give the tenth unto thee.

Summary

vv. 1–2

Isaac sends Jacob to Padan-aram to the house of Bethuel, who is Rebekah's father. Isaac instructs Jacob to choose a wife from Laban's daughters. Laban is Rebekah's brother. Isaac does not want Jacob to marry Canaanite women.

vv. 3–5

Isaac blesses Jacob before he leaves. Isaac directly blesses Jacob with the blessings that God gave to Abraham. Jacob travels toward Padan-aram.

vv. 6–9

Esau sees that Isaac sent Jacob to Padan-aram to get a wife instead of marrying a woman from Canaan. When Esau discovers that his parents are not pleased with Canaanite women, he takes a wife from the family of Ishmael (who is also Abraham's son), hoping this wife will be more pleasing to his parents.

vv. 10–15

On his way to Padan-aram, Jacob stops to sleep because the sun has gone down and takes stones and makes himself a pillow. He has a dream of a ladder that goes from the earth to heaven, and angels are descending and ascending the ladder. The Lord speaks to him and identifies Himself as the God of Abraham and Isaac and states He will give Jacob's descendants this land.

vv. 16–19

When Jacob wakes up from the dream, he takes the stones that were his pillows and pours oil over them. He calls the place *Bethel*, which means "house of God."[61]

vv. 20–22

Jacob makes a vow to God. Jacob vows to make the Lord God his God if God provides for him and brings him back to his father's house in peace. Jacob also promises to give a tenth of his possessions to God.

Commentary

Isaac instructs Jacob to go to Padan-aram to Rebekah's family to choose a wife instead of choosing a wife from the Canaanites. Isaac's desire for Jacob not to marry a Canaanite woman is not because of racial prejudice but because Isaac wants Jacob to marry someone of similar religious beliefs. This is similar to what Abraham did to find a wife for Isaac, except Abraham did not want Isaac to go back to that land, but Jacob was sent there. Isaac also blesses Jacob before he leaves. The statements of blessings given by Isaac to Jacob to "make thee fruitful and multiply thee" and that his seed "mayest be a multitude of people" are similar to the statements that God gave to Abraham.

Although Esau has lost his birthright and his blessing to Jacob, he still desires the approval of his parents, and he is still competing with Jacob for their parents' approval. In response, Esau marries one of Ishmael's daughters in an attempt to gain favor with his parents.

---

[61] The Holy Bible, King James Version (Grand Rapids: Zondervan, 2010).

The experience that Jacob has on his way to Padan-aram is one of the transitions in his life. This is the first time that God talks directly to Jacob. God establishes the covenant blessing of Abraham with Jacob, and Jacob makes a vow to the Lord that the Lord will be his God and that Jacob will pay a tithe. Jacob promises to give God a tenth of his possessions because he is relying on God's promise to take care of him and give him the land that he is currently just a stranger in. Once again, these are similar blessings and promises to those given to Abraham and Isaac.

Many Christians do not believe tithing is necessary or biblically accurate, but we can see from Genesis that both Abraham and Jacob gave a tenth of their possessions to God. This is still a principle that should be applied today. All that we are able to obtain comes from God. Just like Jacob, we rely on Him to fulfill His promise to provide for all of our needs, so we should be willing to give a tenth of it back to God.

Review
1. Compare and contrast Genesis 28:1–5 to Genesis 24:1–5.
2. Discuss Genesis. 28:3–4 in reference to Genesis 12:2–3, 17:8, and 22:17.
3. How does Esau respond to Isaac sending Jacob away to find a wife among Rebekah's relatives?
4. Discuss Jacob's dream.
5. What vow does Jacob make to God when he wakes from his dream?

Genesis Chapter 29

1   Then Jacob went on his journey, and came into the land of the people of the east.

    2 And he looked, and behold a well in the field, and, lo, there were three flocks of sheep lying by it; for out of that well they watered the flocks: and a great stone was upon the well's mouth.

    3 And thither were all the flocks gathered: and they rolled the stone from the well's mouth, and watered the sheep, and put the stone again upon the well's mouth in his place.

    4 And Jacob said unto them, My brethren, whence be ye? And they said, Of Haran are we.

    5 And he said unto them, Know ye Laban the son of Nahor? And they said, We know him.

    6 And he said unto them, Is he well? And they said, He is well: and, behold, Rachel his daughter cometh with the sheep.

    7 And he said, Lo, it is yet high day, neither is it time that the cattle should be gathered together: water ye the sheep, and go and feed them.

    8 And they said, We cannot, until all the flocks be gathered together, and till they roll the stone from the well's mouth; then we water the sheep.

    9 And while he yet spake with them, Rachel came with her father's sheep: for she kept them.

    10 And it came to pass, when Jacob saw Rachel the daughter of Laban his mother's brother, and the sheep of Laban his mother's brother, that Jacob went

near, and rolled the stone from the well's mouth, and watered the flock of Laban his mother's brother.

11 And Jacob kissed Rachel, and lifted up his voice, and wept.

12 And Jacob told Rachel that he was her father's brother, and that he was Rebekah's son: and she ran and told her father.

13 And it came to pass, when Laban heard the tidings of Jacob his sister's son, that he ran to meet him, and embraced him, and kissed him, and brought him to his house. And he told Laban all these things.

14 And Laban said to him, Surely thou art my bone and my flesh. And he abode with him the space of a month.

15 And Laban said unto Jacob, Because thou art my brother, shouldest thou therefore serve me for nought? tell me, what shall thy wages be?

16 And Laban had two daughters: the name of the elder was Leah, and the name of the younger was Rachel.

17 Leah was tender eyed; but Rachel was beautiful and well favoured.

18 And Jacob loved Rachel; and said, I will serve thee seven years for Rachel thy younger daughter.

19 And Laban said, It is better that I give her to thee, than that I should give her to another man: abide with me.

20 And Jacob served seven years for Rachel; and they seemed unto him but a few days, for the love he had to her.

21 And Jacob said unto Laban, Give me my wife, for my days are fulfilled, that I may go in unto her.

22 And Laban gathered together all the men of the place, and made a feast.

23 And it came to pass in the evening, that he took Leah his daughter, and brought her to him; and he went in unto her.

24 And Laban gave unto his daughter Leah Zilpah his maid for an handmaid.

25 And it came to pass, that in the morning, behold, it was Leah: and he said to Laban, What is this thou hast done unto me? did not I serve with thee for Rachel? wherefore then hast thou beguiled me?

26 And Laban said, It must not be so done in our country, to give the younger before the firstborn.

27 Fulfil her week, and we will give thee this also for the service which thou shalt serve with me yet seven other years.

28 And Jacob did so, and fulfilled her week: and he gave him Rachel his daughter to wife also.

29 And Laban gave to Rachel his daughter Bilhah his handmaid to be her maid.

30 And he went in also unto Rachel, and he loved also Rachel more than Leah, and served with him yet seven other years.

31 And when the LORD saw that Leah was hated, he opened her womb: but Rachel was barren.

32 And Leah conceived, and bare a son, and she called his name Reuben: for she said, Surely the LORD hath looked upon my affliction; now therefore my husband will love me.

33 And she conceived again, and bare a son; and said, Because the LORD hath heard that I was hated, he hath therefore given me this son also: and she called his name Simeon.

34 And she conceived again, and bare a son; and said, Now this time will my husband be joined unto me, because I have born him three sons: therefore was his name called Levi.

35 And she conceived again, and bare a son: and she said, Now will I praise the LORD: therefore she called his name Judah; and left bearing.

Summary

vv. 1–8

Jacob arrives at Padan-aram and inquires about Laban. There are shepherds around a well waiting for the stone to be rolled away so they can feed their flock. The shepherds state that Laban is well, and his daughter Rachel arrives to feed the sheep of her father, which she takes care of.

vv. 9–14

While he is still talking to the shepherds, Rachel comes with the sheep. Jacob rolls the rock away and waters the sheep. Jacob identifies himself, and Rachel takes him back home where he meets his uncle Laban. Jacob tells Laban everything that has happened, and Laban greets Jacob warmly.

vv. 15–30

After Jacob has been at Laban's for one month, Laban asks Jacob what he would like for wages. Jacob responds by stating that he will work for seven years to marry Rachel. Laban agrees and states that it would be better for him to give Rachel to Jacob (a relative) than to one of the men in Padan-aram. After the seven years, Jacob asks for Rachel. Laban hosts a large wedding feast, but Laban brings Leah to Jacob as his wife instead of Rachel. When Jacob gets up in the morning, he realizes it is Leah and not Rachel. He asks Laban why he tricked him. Laban explains the deception by stating that it is their custom to give the oldest daughter in marriage before the younger. Laban asks Jacob to fulfill Leah's wedding week and says he will give Jacob Rachel as his wife also. Jacob agrees, and after a week, Rachel is given to Jacob to be his wife. Then Jacob works seven more years for Rachel.

vv. 31–35

Jacob favors Rachel over Leah. Because Jacob does not love Leah, God opens her womb, but Rachel is barren. Leah has four sons named Reuben, Simeon, Levi, and Judah. After having the four sons, God stops her from bearing children temporarily.

Commentary

This chapter begins with Jacob meeting Rachel at a well, which is similar to how Abraham's servant found Rebekah at the well. Laban is initially very welcoming of Jacob and describes him in verse 14 as "my bone and my flesh," similar to when Adam sees Eve. This denotes that Laban recognizes Jacob as a close relative and that there is a "covenant" between relatives.

Now Jacob has met someone who is a better "deceiver or trickster" than he is. When Jacob deceived his father into blessing him instead of Esau, he and his mother put great detail into how the deception was to take place. Isaac was old, and his eyesight was not as good, so Jacob and Rebekah were able to take advantage of this. In this case, Jacob is deceived with his "eyes wide open." Jacob asks Laban why he has "beguiled" him. *Beguiled* means "to deceive by being charming."[62] This is the same term that Eve used when she was tricked by the devil (Genesis 3:13). The serpent told Eve what she wanted to hear, and she was deceived. Laban deceives Jacob so he will have a husband for each of his daughters.

We continue to see sibling rivalry and favoritism. Jacob loves Rachel more than her sister, Leah. The author also makes it clear that Rachel is more physically attractive than Leah. Because Leah is hated, God opens her womb, but Rachel is barren. Despite her outward appearance and the fact that her husband does not love her, God still blesses her to have children. At this point, Leah has four sons. The first is *Reuben*, which means "see a son."[63] Next is *Simeon*, which means "hearing."[64] The third is *Levi*, which means "joined."[65] The fourth is *Judah*, which means "praise."[66] The Levites become the tribe of priests and also the tribe of Moses and Aaron.[67] King David and, of course, Jesus come from the tribe of Judah.[68]

---

[62] "Beguiled," www.thefreedictionary.com.
[63] The Holy Bible, King James Version (Grand Rapids: Zondervan, 2010).
[64] Ibid.
[65] Ibid.
[66] Ibid.
[67] Exodus 2, Exodus 4:14, Leviticus 21
[68] Matthew 1

Review
1. How does Jacob meet Rachel?
2. Discuss Genesis 29:14 in reference to Genesis 2:23.
3. What agreement do Jacob and Laban make so that Jacob can marry Rachel?
4. How is Jacob "tricked" into marrying Leah?
5. What does Rachel have in common with both Sarah and Rebekah?

Genesis Chapter 30

1 And when Rachel saw that she bare Jacob no children, Rachel envied her sister; and said unto Jacob, Give me children, or else I die.

2 And Jacob's anger was kindled against Rachel: and he said, Am I in God's stead, who hath withheld from thee the fruit of the womb?

3 And she said, Behold my maid Bilhah, go in unto her; and she shall bear upon my knees, that I may also have children by her.

4 And she gave him Bilhah her handmaid to wife: and Jacob went in unto her.

5 And Bilhah conceived, and bare Jacob a son.

6 And Rachel said, God hath judged me, and hath also heard my voice, and hath given me a son: therefore called she his name Dan.

7 And Bilhah Rachel's maid conceived again, and bare Jacob a second son.

8 And Rachel said, With great wrestlings have I wrestled with my sister, and I have prevailed: and she called his name Naphtali.

9 When Leah saw that she had left bearing, she took Zilpah her maid, and gave her Jacob to wife.

10 And Zilpah Leah's maid bare Jacob a son.

11 And Leah said, A troop cometh: and she called his name Gad.

12 And Zilpah Leah's maid bare Jacob a second son.

13 And Leah said, Happy am I, for the daughters will call me blessed: and she called his name Asher.

14 And Reuben went in the days of wheat harvest, and found mandrakes in the field, and brought them unto his mother Leah. Then Rachel said to Leah, Give me, I pray thee, of thy son's mandrakes.

15 And she said unto her, Is it a small matter that thou hast taken my husband? and wouldest thou take away my son's mandrakes also? And Rachel said, Therefore he shall lie with thee to night for thy son's mandrakes.

16 And Jacob came out of the field in the evening, and Leah went out to meet him, and said, Thou must come in unto me; for surely I have hired thee with my son's mandrakes. And he lay with her that night.

17 And God hearkened unto Leah, and she conceived, and bare Jacob the fifth son.

18 And Leah said, God hath given me my hire, because I have given my maiden to my husband: and she called his name Issachar.

19 And Leah conceived again, and bare Jacob the sixth son.

20 And Leah said, God hath endued me with a good dowry; now will my husband dwell with me, because I have born him six sons: and she called his name Zebulun.

21 And afterwards she bare a daughter, and called her name Dinah.

22 And God remembered Rachel, and God hearkened to her, and opened her womb.

23 And she conceived, and bare a son; and said, God hath taken away my reproach:

24 And she called his name Joseph; and said, The LORD shall add to me another son.

25 And it came to pass, when Rachel had born Joseph, that Jacob said unto Laban, Send me away, that I may go unto mine own place, and to my country.

26 Give me my wives and my children, for whom I have served thee, and let me go: for thou knowest my service which I have done thee.

27 And Laban said unto him, I pray thee, if I have found favour in thine eyes, tarry: for I have learned by experience that the LORD hath blessed me for thy sake.

28 And he said, Appoint me thy wages, and I will give it.

29 And he said unto him, Thou knowest how I have served thee, and how thy cattle was with me.

30 For it was little which thou hadst before I came, and it is now increased unto a multitude; and the LORD hath blessed thee since my coming: and now when shall I provide for mine own house also?

31 And he said, What shall I give thee? And Jacob said, Thou shalt not give me any thing: if thou wilt do this thing for me, I will again feed and keep thy flock.

32 I will pass through all thy flock to day, removing from thence all the speckled and spotted cattle, and all the brown cattle among the sheep, and the spotted and speckled among the goats: and of such shall be my hire.

33 So shall my righteousness answer for me in time to come, when it shall come for my hire before thy face: every one that is not speckled and spotted among the goats, and brown among the sheep, that shall be counted stolen with me.

34 And Laban said, Behold, I would it might be according to thy word.

35 And he removed that day the he goats that were ringstraked and spotted, and all the she goats that were speckled and spotted, and every one that had some white in it, and all the brown among the sheep, and gave them into the hand of his sons.

36 And he set three days' journey betwixt himself and Jacob: and Jacob fed the rest of Laban's flocks.

37 And Jacob took him rods of green poplar, and of the hazel and chestnut tree; and pilled white strakes in them, and made the white appear which was in the rods.

38 And he set the rods which he had pilled before the flocks in the gutters in the watering troughs when the flocks came to drink, that they should conceive when they came to drink.

39 And the flocks conceived before the rods, and brought forth cattle ringstraked, speckled, and spotted.

40 And Jacob did separate the lambs, and set the faces of the flocks toward the ringstraked, and all the brown in the flock of Laban; and he put his own flocks by themselves, and put them not unto Laban's cattle.

41 And it came to pass, whensoever the stronger cattle did conceive, that Jacob laid the rods before the eyes of the cattle in the gutters, that they might conceive among the rods.

42 But when the cattle were feeble, he put them not in: so the feebler were Laban's, and the stronger Jacob's.

43 And the man increased exceedingly, and had much cattle, and maidservants, and menservants, and camels, and asses.

Summary

vv. 1–2

Rachel is envious of her sister and asks Jacob to give her children. Jacob gets angry with Rachel and tells her that God is the one who gives children, not him.

vv. 3–8

Rachel takes matters into her own hands and gives Jacob her handmaid to be his wife so the children her handmaid will bear can be considered to be Rachel's.

Bilhah, Rachel's handmaid, has two sons. They are *Dan*, which means "he judged" because God judged and vindicated Rachel, and *Naphtali*, which means "wrestled" because Rachel "wrestled" with her sister and won.

vv. 9–13

When Leah sees that she has stopped having children, she gives her handmaid to Jacob as his wife. Zilpah, Leah's handmaid, has two sons. They are *Gad*, which means "good fortune," and *Asher*, which means "happy."

vv. 14–16

Rueben has found mandrakes and brings them to his mother. Rachel asks for the mandrakes. Leah replies by stating that Rachel has already taken her husband and asking if now Rachel wants the mandrakes, too. Rachel receives the mandrakes, but Leah is able to have the night with Jacob. Leah meets Jacob when he is coming out of the field and tells him that he has been bought with her son's mandrakes.

vv. 17–21

God answers Leah's prayer, and she conceives again and has three children. She has two boys and a girl. They are called *Issachar*, which means "hire," *Zebulun*, which means "dwell," and *Dinah*, which means "judgment."[69]

vv. 22–24

God remembers Rachel, and she conceives and has a son named Joseph. *Joseph* means "may he add" or "added."

vv. 25–36

After Joseph is born, Jacob asks Laban for his wages so he can go back to his own land. Laban acknowledges that he has been blessed because of Jacob and does not want him to leave. Laban asks Jacob to tell him what wages he desires. Jacob points out to Laban that he did not have this many cattle before Jacob was working for him and that God has blessed Laban because of him. Jacob states that he would like to have all the speckled and spotted sheep and goats for payment, and he will continue to work for Laban. But that day Laban goes out and takes all the speckled and spotted livestock and puts them in the care of his sons. Laban places a three-day journey between himself and Jacob, but Jacob continues to take care of the rest of Laban's livestock.

---

[69] The Holy Bible, King James Version (Grand Rapids: Zondervan, 2010).

vv. 37–43

Jacob takes poplar, almond, and plane trees and peels them. He places the branches in front of the cattle at the water trough. When the sheep come to drink, they mate and conceive, and they give birth to lambs that are spotted and speckled. Jacob starts to separate his flock from Laban's flock. When the stronger, healthier sheep are breeding, he places the branches in front of them so they will produce strong and healthy offspring. The stronger sheep will end up being Jacob's flock, and the weaker cattle will end up being Laban's flock. Jacob's flock increases.

Commentary

This chapter continues to emphasize the sibling rivalry that is prevalent in this family in that Rachel and Leah are competing for Jacob's love and for their status as wives by the bearing of children. Although Rachel is loved by Jacob, she originally was barren. Because Leah is not loved by Jacob, God makes her fruitful. Rachel asks Jacob to give her children, and Jacob becomes angry with her because he states that God controls fertility. This is significant because, at that time, there was no understanding or knowledge of ovulation. People believed that God made a woman fertile or infertile, and infertility was a punishment or curse for something that one did wrong.

Before Jacob goes to Padan-aram, God promises him many descendants, so it is ironic that the woman Jacob loves and wants to marry is barren, but the woman he does not love is fruitful. It might not be Jacob's plan to marry Leah, but it appears that it is God's plan, because it is through the descendants of her son Judah that Jesus is born. However, Rachel does have two sons, and Rachel's oldest son, Joseph, becomes the "covenant" bearer for the next generation. Rachel's conception is also supernatural because the text emphasizes that God remembers Rachel and opens her womb.

Having a handmaid act as a surrogate for a barren woman and claiming her offspring as the child of the wife was a common practice at that time. We see that Sarah did this also. Because the child born by the handmaid was legally not her child, she had no rights to the child. In this chapter, we see that the handmaids do not name their children, but Leah and Rachel do.[70]

The mandrake is a Mediterranean plant that was used as an aphrodisiac and for fertility.[71] This is why Rachel desires the plant and is willing to give up nights with her husband to obtain the plant. The passage does not record whether Jacob protests. It seems he goes with Leah as he is instructed, almost as if he is a pawn in a game between the sisters.

---

[70] Wenham, *Word Biblical Commentary*, 2:7.
[71] Ibid., 246-247.

In the last chapter, Jacob was deceived by Laban, but now Jacob "deceives" Laban by using this traditional strategy to breed stronger animals for his flock.[72]

Review
1. How do Leah and Rachel use childbearing to gain favor with Jacob?
2. What is a mandrake, and why is it relevant in this chapter?
3. Who is Joseph?
4. What agreement do Laban and Jacob have in regard to Jacob's payment for keeping Laban's flock?
5. How does Laban attempt to "con" Jacob out of his payment?

---

[72] Walton, *Genesis*, 590.

Genesis Chapter 31

1 And he heard the words of Laban's sons, saying, Jacob hath taken away all that was our father's; and of that which was our father's hath he gotten all this glory.

2 And Jacob beheld the countenance of Laban, and, behold, it was not toward him as before.

3 And the LORD said unto Jacob, Return unto the land of thy fathers, and to thy kindred; and I will be with thee.

4 And Jacob sent and called Rachel and Leah to the field unto his flock,

5 And said unto them, I see your father's countenance, that it is not toward me as before; but the God of my father hath been with me.

6 And ye know that with all my power I have served your father.

7 And your father hath deceived me, and changed my wages ten times; but God suffered him not to hurt me.

8 If he said thus, The speckled shall be thy wages; then all the cattle bare speckled: and if he said thus, The ringstraked shall be thy hire; then bare all the cattle ringstraked.

9 Thus God hath taken away the cattle of your father, and given them to me.

10 And it came to pass at the time that the cattle conceived, that I lifted up mine eyes, and saw in a dream, and, behold, the rams which leaped upon the cattle were ringstraked, speckled, and grisled.

11 And the angel of God spake unto me in a dream, saying, Jacob: and I said, Here am I.

12 And he said, Lift up now thine eyes, and see, all the rams which leap upon the cattle are ringstraked, speckled, and grisled: for I have seen all that Laban doeth unto thee.

13 I am the God of Beth-el, where thou anointedst the pillar, and where thou vowedst a vow unto me: now arise, get thee out from this land, and return unto the land of thy kindred.

14 And Rachel and Leah answered and said unto him, Is there yet any portion or inheritance for us in our father's house?

15 Are we not counted of him strangers? for he hath sold us, and hath quite devoured also our money.

16 For all the riches which God hath taken from our father, that is our's, and our children's: now then, whatsoever God hath said unto thee, do.

17 Then Jacob rose up, and set his sons and his wives upon camels;

18 And he carried away all his cattle, and all his goods which he had gotten, the cattle of his getting, which he had gotten in Padan-aram, for to go to Isaac his father in the land of Canaan.

19 And Laban went to shear his sheep: and Rachel had stolen the images that were her father's.

20 And Jacob stole away unawares to Laban the Syrian, in that he told him not that he fled.

21 So he fled with all that he had; and he rose up, and passed over the river, and set his face toward the mount Gilead.

22 And it was told Laban on the third day that Jacob was fled.

23 And he took his brethren with him, and pursued after him seven days' journey; and they overtook him in the mount Gilead.

24 And God came to Laban the Syrian in a dream by night, and said unto him, Take heed that thou speak not to Jacob either good or bad.

25 Then Laban overtook Jacob. Now Jacob had pitched his tent in the mount: and Laban with his brethren pitched in the mount of Gilead.

26 And Laban said to Jacob, What hast thou done, that thou hast stolen away unawares to me, and carried away my daughters, as captives taken with the sword?

27 Wherefore didst thou flee away secretly, and steal away from me; and didst not tell me, that I might have sent thee away with mirth, and with songs, with tabret, and with harp?

28 And hast not suffered me to kiss my sons and my daughters? thou hast now done foolishly in so doing.

29 It is in the power of my hand to do you hurt: but the God of your father spake unto me yesternight, saying, Take thou heed that thou speak not to Jacob either good or bad.

30 And now, though thou wouldest needs be gone, because thou sore longedst after thy father's house, yet wherefore hast thou stolen my gods?

31 And Jacob answered and said to Laban, Because I was afraid: for I said, Peradventure thou wouldest take by force thy daughters from me.

32 With whomsoever thou findest thy gods, let him not live: before our brethren discern thou what is thine with me, and take it to thee. For Jacob knew not that Rachel had stolen them.

33 And Laban went into Jacob's tent, and into Leah's tent, and into the two maidservants' tents; but he found them not. Then went he out of Leah's tent, and entered into Rachel's tent.

34 Now Rachel had taken the images, and put them in the camel's furniture, and sat upon them. And Laban searched all the tent, but found them not.

35 And she said to her father, Let it not displease my lord that I cannot rise up before thee; for the custom of women is upon me. And he searched, but found not the images.

36 And Jacob was wroth, and chode with Laban: and Jacob answered and said to Laban, What is my trespass? what is my sin, that thou hast so hotly pursued after me?

37 Whereas thou hast searched all my stuff, what hast thou found of all thy household stuff? set it here before my brethren and thy brethren, that they may judge betwixt us both.

38 This twenty years have I been with thee; thy ewes and thy she goats have not cast their young, and the rams of thy flock have I not eaten.

39 That which was torn of beasts I brought not unto thee; I bare the loss of it; of my hand didst thou require it, whether stolen by day, or stolen by night.

40 Thus I was; in the day the drought consumed me, and the frost by night; and my sleep departed from mine eyes.

41 Thus have I been twenty years in thy house; I served thee fourteeen years for thy two daughters, and six years for thy cattle: and thou hast changed my wages ten times.

42 Except the God of my father, the God of Abraham, and the fear of Isaac, had been with me, surely thou hadst sent me away now empty. God hath seen mine affliction and the labour of my hands, and rebuked thee yesternight.

43 And Laban answered and said unto Jacob, These daughters are my daughters, and these children are my children, and these cattle are my cattle, and all that thou seest is mine: and what can I do this day unto these my daughters, or unto their children which they have born?

44 Now therefore come thou, let us make a covenant, I and thou; and let it be for a witness between me and thee.

45 And Jacob took a stone, and set it up for a pillar.

46 And Jacob said unto his brethren, Gather stones; and they took stones, and made an heap: and they did eat there upon the heap.

47 And Laban called it Jegar-sahadutha: but Jacob called it Galeed;

48 And Laban said, This heap is a witness between me and thee this day. Therefore was the name of it called Galeed;

49 And Mizpah; for he said, The LORD watch between me and thee, when we are absent one from another.

50 If thou shalt afflict my daughters, or if thou shalt take other wives beside my daughters, no man is with us; see, God is witness betwixt me and thee.

51 And Laban said to Jacob, Behold this heap, and behold this pillar, which I have cast betwixt me and thee;

52 This heap be witness, and this pillar be witness, that I will not pass over this heap to thee, and that thou shalt not pass over this heap and this pillar unto me, for harm.

53 The God of Abraham, and the God of Nahor, the God of their father, judge betwixt us. And Jacob sware by the fear of his father Isaac.

54 Then Jacob offered sacrifice upon the mount, and called his brethren to eat bread: and they did eat bread, and tarried all night in the mount.

55 And early in the morning Laban rose up, and kissed his sons and his daughters, and blessed them: and Laban departed, and returned unto his place.

Summary

vv. 1–16

Laban's sons complain about Jacob and feel that Jacob has become prosperous by stealing their inheritance. Laban no longer looks favorably on Jacob. The Lord tells Jacob to return to the land of his fathers. Jacob has a discussion with Rachel and Leah about leaving. He states that Laban has deceived him and has changed his wages several times, but Jacob has still been faithful to Laban. Jacob tells them that an angel of God has come to him in a dream and has instructed him to leave. In this dream, God identifies himself as the God of Bethel. It was at Bethel that Jacob anointed the pillar of stones and had the dream of angels descending and ascending into heaven. Rachel and Leah reply that they have no inheritance from their father and he has essentially sold them to Jacob. The riches that God has taken from Laban and given to Jacob belong to them and their children, so they agree to go as God has instructed.

vv. 17–32

Jacob, his wives, their handmaids, and his children pack up and leave to go back to Canaan without telling Laban. Laban goes to shear his sheep and is unaware that they have left. Rachel takes her father's images. It is not until three days later that Laban realizes Jacob and his family have left. Laban immediately follows after them and finds them after seven days. But the night before he meets them, God comes to Laban in a dream and tells him not to speak badly to Jacob. Laban finds them in Gilead. Laban asks Jacob why he left without telling Laban like Jacob had been held captive and was running away. Laban states that if Jacob would have said he was leaving that it would have given Laban an opportunity to have a going away celebration for them and to say goodbye to his daughters and grandchildren. Because of the way Jacob left, Laban states he is within his rights to harm him, but God has spoken to him and told him not to speak badly to Jacob. Then Laban states that someone has stolen his images. Jacob responds that he thought if he'd told Laban he was leaving that Laban would have forcibly taken his wives and children. Then Jacob states that Laban is free to search for his images and that whoever has them will die. Jacob is unaware that Rachel has stolen them.

vv. 33–42

Laban searches the tents and does not find the images. When Laban searches Rachel's tent, she is sitting on the images and does not get up because she states she is on her menstrual cycle. Jacob becomes upset because he believes Laban has falsely accused him of taking the images, and Jacob expresses how he feels. Jacob states that he has worked twenty years for Laban. He worked fourteen years for his wives and six years for the livestock, and Laban changed his wages ten times. Jacob concludes by stating that if not for the fact God is with him, Laban would have given him nothing.

vv. 43–55

Laban responds by stating that these are his daughters and grandchildren, and he will not hurt them. Laban and Jacob make a covenant there with a stone pillar. Laban calls it Jegar-sahadutha, but Jacob calls it Galeed. Laban says that Jacob cannot abuse his daughters or take other wives as part of this covenant. Laban will not pass that stone to harm Jacob, and Jacob will not pass that stone to harm Laban. There is no man to witness the covenant, so Jacob swears to this by the God of his father Isaac, and Laban swears by the God of Abraham and Nahor. Jacob offers a sacrifice, and they eat together. Laban rises up the next morning, kisses his daughters and grandchildren, and goes back home.

Commentary

Jacob came to Padan-aram with nothing. He had no wives, no children, and no livestock. He was literally running for his life. Because Jacob was his nephew, Laban allowed him to work for him. Although Laban did deceive him by giving him Leah first instead of Rachel, they otherwise seem to have a good relationship. But when Jacob's flock begins to increase and Laban's son complain, there is a strain on the relationship, and Jacob decides to leave. Jacob and his family leave without telling Laban, and when Laban finds out, he pursues them with evil intentions. Jacob originally fled to Padan-aram, and now he is fleeing back to Canaan. God is still with Jacob and protecting him because God comes to Laban before he confronts Jacob and warns Laban not to speak badly toward Jacob.

I believe that the author recorded Rachel's theft of the idols for several reasons. Rachel still has a belief in idol gods, so these items were valuable to her. We also see that she is a deceiver just like her husband and father because she lies about having them. Although Rachel does not die at this time, Rachel does die later in childbirth, and Jacob states that anyone who has the idols will die.

Laban and Jacob come to an agreement. Laban makes Jacob vow that he will be a good husband to his daughters and take no other wives. Although we do not see anywhere else in this story that Laban is a loving father, he appears to care about protecting his offspring both physically and financially. Because there are no witnesses to this covenant, a higher authority has to be a witness. Jacob swears by the God of his father, Isaac. But Laban swears by the God of Abraham and the god of Nahor because Laban is an idol worshipper and believes in many gods.[73] Despite Laban's history of being a deceiver, it seems that he does keep his part of the agreement, and there is no further conflict recorded between Laban and Jacob.

Review
1. What influences Jacob to have a discussion with Leah and Rachel about leaving Padan-aram?
2. What is Leah and Rachel's response to leaving Padan-aram?
3. Who steals Laban's idols? Discuss their significance.
4. What does God say to Laban about Jacob? Does it influence Laban's treatment of Jacob? If so, how?
5. How do Laban and Jacob finally part?

---

[73] Wenham, *Word Biblical Commentary*, 2: 280-281.

Genesis Chapter 32

1   *And Jacob went on his way, and the angels of God met him.*
2 And when Jacob saw them, he said, This is God's host: and he called the name of that place Mahanaim.

3 And Jacob sent messengers before him to Esau his brother unto the land of Seir, the country of Edom.

4 And he commanded them, saying, Thus shall ye speak unto my lord Esau; Thy servant Jacob saith thus, I have sojourned with Laban, and stayed there until now:

5 And I have oxen, and asses, flocks, and menservants, and womenservants: and I have sent to tell my lord, that I may find grace in thy sight.

6 And the messengers returned to Jacob, saying, We came to thy brother Esau, and also he cometh to meet thee, and four hundred men with him.

7 Then Jacob was greatly afraid and distressed: and he divided the people that was with him, and the flocks, and herds, and the camels, into two bands;

8 And said, If Esau come to the one company, and smite it, then the other company which is left shall escape.

9 And Jacob said, O God of my father Abraham, and God of my father Isaac, the LORD which saidst unto me, Return unto thy country, and to thy kindred, and I will deal well with thee:

10 I am not worthy of the least of all the mercies, and of all the truth, which thou hast shewed unto thy servant; for with my staff I passed over this Jordan, and now I am become two bands.

11 Deliver me, I pray thee, from the hand of my brother, from the hand of Esau: for I fear him, lest he will come and smite me, and the mother with the children.

12 And thou saidst, I will surely do thee good, and make thy seed as the sand of the sea, which cannot be numbered for multitude.

13 And he lodged there that same night; and took of that which came to his hand a present for Esau his brother;

14 Two hundred she goats, and twenty he goats, two hundred ewes, and twenty rams,

15 Thirty milch camels with their colts, forty kine, and ten bulls, twenty she asses, and ten foals.

16 And he delivered them into the hand of his servants, every drove by themselves; and said unto his servants, Pass over before me, and put a space betwixt drove and drove.

17 And he commanded the foremost, saying, When Esau my brother meeteth thee, and asketh thee, saying, Whose art thou? and whither goest thou? and whose are these before thee?

18 Then thou shalt say, They be thy servant Jacob's; it is a present sent unto my lord Esau: and, behold, also he is behind us.

19 And so commanded he the second, and the third, and all that followed the droves, saying, On this manner shall ye speak unto Esau, when ye find him.

20 And say ye moreover, Behold, thy servant Jacob is behind us. For he said, I will appease him with the present that goeth before me, and afterward I will see his face; peradventure he will accept of me.

21 So went the present over before him: and himself lodged that night in the company.

22 And he rose up that night, and took his two wives, and his two womenservants, and his eleven sons, and passed over the ford Jabbok.

23 And he took them, and sent them over the brook, and sent over that he had.

24 And Jacob was left alone; and there wrestled a man with him until the breaking of the day.

25 And when he saw that he prevailed not against him, he touched the hollow of his thigh; and the hollow of Jacob's thigh was out of joint, as he wrestled with him.

26 And he said, Let me go, for the day breaketh. And he said, I will not let thee go, except thou bless me.

27 And he said unto him, What is thy name? And he said, Jacob.

28 And he said, Thy name shall be called no more Jacob, but Israel: for as a prince hast thou power with God and with men, and hast prevailed.

29 And Jacob asked him, and said, Tell me, I pray thee, thy name. And he said, Wherefore is it that thou dost ask after my name? And he blessed him there.

30 And Jacob called the name of the place Peniel: for I have seen God face to face, and my life is preserved.

31 And as he passed over Penuel the sun rose upon him, and he halted upon his thigh.

32 Therefore the children of Israel eat not of the sinew which shrank, which is upon the hollow of the thigh, unto this day: because he touched the hollow of Jacob's thigh in the sinew that shrank.

Summary
vv. 1–8

As Jacob is traveling back to Canaan, the angels of God meet him, and he calls that place Mahanaim. Jacob sends messengers to Esau with a greeting and a message stating that he has been staying with Laban. The Lord has blessed him with cattle and servants. Jacob sends a gift to Esau, hoping he will show Jacob favor. The messenger returns and states Esau is coming to meet him with four hundred men. Jacob becomes afraid and divides his possessions into two separate divisions. He rationalizes that if one division is overtaken, then the other will be able to escape.

vv. 9–20

Jacob prays to God. He addresses God as the God of Abraham, Isaac, and the God that told him to return to Canaan. Jacob states he is not worthy of God's mercy, but he asks God to protect him from Esau. Jacob reminds God that He said He would do good to Jacob and that He would multiply Jacob's seed as the sand on the seashore. Jacob sends Esau a gift of a large number of livestock by way of his servants. Jacob instructs his servants to keep a large distance between them and Jacob. He tells his servants to tell Esau this is a present and that Jacob is following behind them. Jacob's plan is to present the gifts first and then follow with the hope that Esau will accept his gift and greet him peacefully.

vv. 21–32

Jacob sends his wives, handmaids, and children to Jabbok on the other side of the brook, and Jacob camps by himself. While Jacob is alone, he wrestles with a man all night. When the man realizes he is not winning, he touches Jacob's hip and places it out of joint. The man asks Jacob to let him go, but Jacob states that he will not let him go until the man blesses him. The man asks Jacob what his name is, and Jacob replies with his name. At this point, the man (angel) changes

Jacob's name to *Israel*, which means "prince which prevails."[74] Jacob asks the man (angel) what his name is, and the man replies by asking, "Why do you ask me my name?" The man (angel) blesses Jacob. Jacob names this place *Peniel* because he has seen God face to face. Because of this event, the Jewish people do not eat the hollow of an animal's thigh.

Commentary

Although it has been twenty years since they have seen each other, Jacob is still concerned that Esau might be angry about Jacob stealing his blessing, and Jacob worries that Esau desires to take revenge. Jacob sends gifts to Esau in hopes that he will receive Jacob in peace. As a precaution, Jacob divides his possessions and sends his wives and children to a safer location to prepare for a potential conflict with Esau.

The man who wrestles with Jacob represents God. This is another example of a theophany. Jacob even names the area *Peniel*, which means "the face of God." Jacob's name change is similar to when God changed Abram's name to Abraham. Jacob is no longer a deceiver, but now he is the prince of God. The change of Jacob's name signifies a change of character and purpose. Although Abraham is considered the father of the Jewish people, they are called Israelites, and their current nation is Israel, not Abraham, which emphasizes the importance of Jacob's name change.

Review

1. What message does Jacob send to Esau?
2. How does Jacob respond to the messenger's report about Esau?
3. What present does Jacob offer Esau?
4. Describe what happens when Jacob wrestles with the angel.
5. Why is Jacob's name changed?

---

[74] The Holy Bible, King James Version (Grand Rapids: Zondervan, 2010).

Genesis Chapter 33

1 *And Jacob lifted up his eyes, and looked, and, behold, Esau came, and with him four hundred men. And he divided the children unto Leah, and unto Rachel, and unto the two handmaids.*

2 And he put the handmaids and their children foremost, and Leah and her children after, and Rachel and Joseph hindermost.

3 And he passed over before them, and bowed himself to the ground seven times, until he came near to his brother.

4 And Esau ran to meet him, and embraced him, and fell on his neck, and kissed him: and they wept.

5 And he lifted up his eyes, and saw the women and the children; and said, Who are those with thee? And he said, The children which God hath graciously given thy servant.

6 Then the handmaidens came near, they and their children, and they bowed themselves.

7 And Leah also with her children came near, and bowed themselves: and after came Joseph near and Rachel, and they bowed themselves.

8 And he said, What meanest thou by all this drove which I met? And he said, These are to find grace in the sight of my lord.

9 And Esau said, I have enough, my brother; keep that thou hast unto thyself.

10 And Jacob said, Nay, I pray thee, if now I have found grace in thy sight, then receive my present at my hand: for therefore I have seen thy face, as though I had seen the face of God, and thou wast pleased with me.

11 Take, I pray thee, my blessing that is brought to thee; because God hath dealt graciously with me, and because I have enough. And he urged him, and he took it.

12 And he said, Let us take our journey, and let us go, and I will go before thee.

13 And he said unto him, My lord knoweth that the children are tender, and the flocks and herds with young are with me: and if men should overdrive them one day, all the flock will die.

14 Let my lord, I pray thee, pass over before his servant: and I will lead on softly, according as the cattle that goeth before me and the children be able to endure, until I come unto my lord unto Seir.

15 And Esau said, Let me now leave with thee some of the folk that are with me. And he said, What needeth it? let me find grace in the sight of my lord.

16 So Esau returned that day on his way unto Seir.

17 And Jacob journeyed to Succoth, and built him an house, and made booths for his cattle: therefore the name of the place is called Succoth.

18 And Jacob came to Shalem, a city of Shechem, which is in the land of Canaan, when he came from Padan-aram; and pitched his tent before the city.

19 And he bought a parcel of a field, where he had spread his tent, at the hand of the children of Hamor, Shechem's father, for an hundred pieces of money.

20 And he erected there an altar, and called it El-elohe-Israel.

Summary

vv. 1–2

Jacob sees Esau coming toward him with four hundred men. He arranges his family with his handmaids and their children first, then Leah and her children, and finally Rachel and Joseph.

vv. 3–11

Jacob bows seven times when he is close to his brother. Esau hugs and kisses Jacob. He asks Jacob who the people with him are. Jacob responds that they are his children. The handmaids, Leah, Rachel, and their children all bow to Esau. Esau asks about all the livestock that were sent. Jacob replies that they were a gift. Esau declines because he states that he has plenty himself. Jacob insists Esau take them, so Esau finally accepts Jacob's gift.

vv. 12–16

Esau says he will lead the way back to Canaan. Jacob states that he will follow since his livestock cannot move fast because they need to drink water and graze. Also, Jacob states he has young children who cannot travel fast. Esau agrees and offers to leave some men with Jacob to protect him, but Jacob refuses. Esau travels back to Seir.

vv. 17–20
Jacob returns to Canaan by going through Succoth to Shechem and buys land and settles there.

Commentary

When Jacob prepares to meet Esau, he organized his wives and children from "least" favorite or important to "most" favorite. This once again lets the reader know that favoritism is prevalent in almost every situation with this family.

The meeting of Esau is anticlimactic. Jacob expects a confrontation, but the exact opposite occurs. Esau and Jacob finally meet, and the greeting is friendly. It appears that Esau is no longer angry and is not trying to seek revenge. It is not recorded that Jacob and Esau ever meet again, except when they bury their father, Isaac. Although all seems well between Esau and Jacob, Jacob still does not fully trust Esau and decides to settle in a different area. But as far as what is recorded in the Bible, it appears as if Esau has changed and has forgiven Jacob. Despite this pleasant reunion, the descendants of Jacob (Israelites) and Esau (Edomites) continue to have conflict until eventually, God says He will punish and destroy Edom.[75]

Review
1. How does Jacob organize his wives, their handmaids, and his children when preparing to meet Esau?
2. What is Esau's response when he finally greets Jacob?
3. Why does Jacob offer Esau presents? What is Esau's response to Jacob's gifts?
4. Why doesn't Jacob allow Esau to escort him back to Canaan?
5. Does the Bible record whether Jacob and Esau ever see each other again?

---

[75] Obadiah 1-15

Genesis Chapter 34

1   *And Dinah the daughter of Leah, which she bare unto Jacob, went out to see the daughters of the land.*

2 And when Shechem the son of Hamor the Hivite, prince of the country, saw her, he took her, and lay with her, and defiled her.

3 And his soul clave unto Dinah the daughter of Jacob, and he loved the damsel, and spake kindly unto the damsel.

4 And Shechem spake unto his father Hamor, saying, Get me this damsel to wife.

5 And Jacob heard that he had defiled Dinah his daughter: now his sons were with his cattle in the field: and Jacob held his peace until they were come.

6 And Hamor the father of Shechem went out unto Jacob to commune with him.

7 And the sons of Jacob came out of the field when they heard it: and the men were grieved, and they were very wroth, because he had wrought folly in Israel in lying with Jacob's daughter; which thing ought not to be done.

8 And Hamor communed with them, saying, The soul of my son Shechem longeth for your daughter: I pray you give her him to wife.

9 And make ye marriages with us, and give your daughters unto us, and take our daughters unto you.

10 And ye shall dwell with us: and the land shall be before you; dwell and trade ye therein, and get you possessions therein.

11 And Shechem said unto her father and unto her brethren, Let me find grace in your eyes, and what ye shall say unto me I will give.

12 Ask me never so much dowry and gift, and I will give according as ye shall say unto me: but give me the damsel to wife.

13 And the sons of Jacob answered Shechem and Hamor his father deceitfully, and said, because he had defiled Dinah their sister:

14 And they said unto them, We cannot do this thing, to give our sister to one that is uncircumcised; for that were a reproach unto us:

15 But in this will we consent unto you: If ye will be as we be, that every male of you be circumcised;

16 Then will we give our daughters unto you, and we will take your daughters to us, and we will dwell with you, and we will become one people.

17 But if ye will not hearken unto us, to be circumcised; then will we take our daughter, and we will be gone.

18 And their words pleased Hamor, and Shechem Hamor's son.

19 And the young man deferred not to do the thing, because he had delight in Jacob's daughter: and he was more honourable than all the house of his father.

20 And Hamor and Shechem his son came unto the gate of their city, and communed with the men of their city, saying,

21 These men are peaceable with us; therefore let them dwell in the land, and trade therein; for the land, behold, it is large enough for them; let us take their daughters to us for wives, and let us give them our daughters.

22 Only herein will the men consent unto us for to dwell with us, to be one people, if every male among us be circumcised, as they are circumcised.

23 Shall not their cattle and their substance and every beast of their's be ours? only let us consent unto them, and they will dwell with us.

24 And unto Hamor and unto Shechem his son hearkened all that went out of the gate of his city; and every male was circumcised, all that went out of the gate of his city.

25 And it came to pass on the third day, when they were sore, that two of the sons of Jacob, Simeon and Levi, Dinah's brethren, took each man his sword, and came upon the city boldly, and slew all the males.

26 And they slew Hamor and Shechem his son with the edge of the sword, and took Dinah out of Shechem's house, and went out.

27 The sons of Jacob came upon the slain, and spoiled the city, because they had defiled their sister.

28 They took their sheep, and their oxen, and their asses, and that which was in the city, and that which was in the field,

29 And all their wealth, and all their little ones, and their wives took they captive, and spoiled even all that was in the house.

30 And Jacob said to Simeon and Levi, Ye have troubled me to make me to stink among the inhabitants of the land, among the Canaanites and the Perizzites: and I being few in number, they shall gather themselves together against me, and slay me; and I shall be destroyed, I and my house.

31 And they said, Should he deal with our sister as with an harlot?

Summary

vv. 1–4

Dinah, the daughter of Jacob and Leah, goes out to socialize with the other young ladies of the area. The prince called Shechem (which is also the name of the country) sees her, desires her, and sexually assaults her. After he assaults her, he realizes he loves her and desires to marry her. He asks his father, Hamor, to get Dinah for his wife.

vv. 5–23

Jacob discovers that Shechem has sexually assaulted Dinah, and does not say anything to his sons. Shechem and Hamor come to visit with Jacob. Jacob's sons hear what happened and are very angry. Shechem and Hamor approach Jacob and his sons to ask if Dinah can become Shechem's wife. They also say that Jacob's family can settle there and that they can intermarry, trade, and become one nation. Shechem states he will give them whatever they ask as a dowry gift. Jacob's sons answer deceitfully because they have no intention of giving Dinah to be Shechem's wife because he has sexually assaulted her. Jacob replies that all their men have to be circumcised. If they agree to this, then Jacob will agree to give Dinah as Shechem's wife and to dwell there in peace and intermarry as one people. Shechem and Hamor agree. They tell the men of Shechem about the terms of the agreement with Jacob's family, and the men of Shechem approve.

vv. 24–31

The men of Shechem circumcise themselves, and while they are still recovering, Simeon and Levi (full brothers of Dinah) go into the city and kill all the men. They remove Dinah from Shechem's house. They take the women and children captive and take all the possessions of the people of Shechem. When Jacob discovers what Simeon and Levi have done, he is angry with them because the inhabitants of the land will not look favorably on them. The land is inhabited by Canaanites and Perizzites, and Jacob's family is small in comparison to the other inhabitants of the land. Jacob thinks the other inhabitants will band together and kill them all. Simeon and Levi's response is to question whether they should allow their sister to be treated like a prostitute.

Commentary

This chapter seems out of place because it does not continue with the story of Jacob but describes a story about Dinah. Although the sexual assault of Dinah is the catalyst for the rest of the events in the chapter, she is not the primary character. The men are still the central figures, and all the decisions are made by them. Dinah is simply a pawn in this chapter. First, she is sexually assaulted by Shechem. Then she is used as an excuse for her brothers to kill a people and take their possessions.

I do not believe that Jacob is being insensitive toward Dinah in that she does not deserve vindication, but Jacob is now thinking about preserving his family. Also, Simeon and Levi's actions are extremely violent in that not only do they kill the man responsible, but they kill all the men in the city. Although their actions are violent and could cause danger to the family, Simeon and Levi think they are justified because they are protecting their sister's honor. Jacob references this incident when he gives blessings to Simeon and Levi in Genesis 49.

Review

1. After Shechem defiles Dinah, what request does he make of his father?
2. How do Dinah's brothers feel about what Shechem has done to her?
3. What agreement do Jacob and his sons make with Shechem and Hamor?
4. What do Levi and Simeon do to the males of Shechem?
5. How do the events in this chapter relate to the blessings in Genesis 49?

Genesis Chapter 35

1 And God said unto Jacob, Arise, go up to Beth-el, and dwell there: and make there an altar unto God, that appeared unto thee when thou fleddest from the face of Esau thy brother.

2 Then Jacob said unto his household, and to all that were with him, Put away the strange gods that are among you, and be clean, and change your garments:

3 And let us arise, and go up to Beth-el; and I will make there an altar unto God, who answered me in the day of my distress, and was with me in the way which I went.

4 And they gave unto Jacob all the strange gods which were in their hand, and all their earrings which were in their ears; and Jacob hid them under the oak which was by Shechem.

5 And they journeyed: and the terror of God was upon the cities that were round about them, and they did not pursue after the sons of Jacob.

6 So Jacob came to Luz, which is in the land of Canaan, that is, Beth-el, he and all the people that were with him.

7 And he built there an altar, and called the place El-beth-el: because there God appeared unto him, when he fled from the face of his brother.

8 But Deborah Rebekah's nurse died, and she was buried beneath Beth-el under an oak: and the name of it was called Allon-bachuth.

9 And God appeared unto Jacob again, when he came out of Padan-aram, and blessed him.

10 And God said unto him, Thy name is Jacob: thy name shall not be called any more Jacob, but Israel shall be thy name: and he called his name Israel.

11 And God said unto him, I am God Almighty: be fruitful and multiply; a nation and a company of nations shall be of thee, and kings shall come out of thy loins;

12 And the land which I gave Abraham and Isaac, to thee I will give it, and to thy seed after thee will I give the land.

13 And God went up from him in the place where he talked with him.

14 And Jacob set up a pillar in the place where he talked with him, even a pillar of stone: and he poured a drink offering thereon, and he poured oil thereon.

15 And Jacob called the name of the place where God spake with him, Beth-el.

16 And they journeyed from Beth-el; and there was but a little way to come to Ephrath: and Rachel travailed, and she had hard labour.

17 And it came to pass, when she was in hard labour, that the midwife said unto her, Fear not; thou shalt have this son also.

18 And it came to pass, as her soul was in departing, (for she died) that she called his name Ben-oni: but his father called him Benjamin.

19 And Rachel died, and was buried in the way to Ephrath, which is Beth-lehem.

20 And Jacob set a pillar upon her grave: that is the pillar of Rachel's grave unto this day.

21 And Israel journeyed, and spread his tent beyond the tower of Edar.

22 And it came to pass, when Israel dwelt in that land, that Reuben went and lay with Bilhah his father's concubine: and Israel heard it. Now the sons of Jacob were twelve:

23 The sons of Leah; Reuben, Jacob's firstborn, and Simeon, and Levi, and Judah, and Issachar, and Zebulun:

24 The sons of Rachel; Joseph, and Benjamin:

25 And the sons of Bilhah, Rachel's handmaid; Dan, and Naphtali:

26 And the sons of Zilpah, Leah's handmaid; Gad, and Asher: these are the sons of Jacob, which were born to him in Padan-aram.

27 And Jacob came unto Isaac his father unto Mamre, unto the city of Arbah, which is Hebron, where Abraham and Isaac sojourned.

28 And the days of Isaac were an hundred and fourscore years.

29 And Isaac gave up the ghost, and died, and was gathered unto his people, being old and full of days: and his sons Esau and Jacob buried him.

Summary

vv. 1–8

God tells Jacob to go to Bethel, where he had built an altar to God after fleeing from Esau. Jacob instructs his family to put away all foreign gods and to change their clothes. Jacob takes all their gods and earrings and hides them under an oak tree in Shechem. As they travel to Bethel, God puts fear in the surrounding people so they will not attack Jacob's family. Once Jacob arrives in Bethel, he builds an altar. Also, Deborah, Rebekah's nurse, dies there.

vv. 9–15

God appears to Jacob again. God repeats that Jacob's name is changed to Israel. God identifies Himself as God Almighty, tells Jacob to be fruitful and multiply, says He will make Israel a great nation, and promises that there will be kings from Jacob's descendants. God states that the land He promised to Abraham and Isaac will be given to Jacob's descendants. Jacob makes an altar there and presents an offering at Bethel.

vv. 16–21

Rachel goes into labor but dies during childbirth. Rachel names their son *Ben-oni*, which means "the son of my sorrow," but Jacob names him *Benjamin*, which means "the son of the right hand." Rachel is buried, and Jacob sets up a pillar on her grave in Bethlehem.

v. 22

Reuben has sexual relations with Jacob's handmaid, Bilhah.

vv. 23–26

This is a record of all of Jacob's sons.
The sons of Leah are Reuben, Simeon, Levi, Judah, Issachar, and Zebulun.
The sons of Rachel are Joseph and Benjamin.
The sons of Bilhah are Dan and Naphtali.
The sons of Zilpah are Gad and Asher.

vv. 27–29

Jacob goes to Mamre, where Abraham and Isaac lived. Isaac dies at 180 years old. Esau and Jacob bury Isaac.

Commentary

Before Jacob returns to Bethel, where he originally experienced his first personal encounter with God, he purifies his family by removing all foreign gods and having them change their clothes. Obviously, getting rid of the foreign gods relates to Jacob's vow that God will be his God if God protects him. God has fulfilled His part of the covenant by protecting Jacob, and Jacob fulfills his part by removing all foreign objects from his family. The changing of their clothes is also a significant part of their purification process.

There are many statements repeated here that God spoke to Abraham and Isaac. First, God repeats that Jacob has a new name, Israel. God states many promises, such as Jacob being fruitful, that Israel will become a nation, and that there will be kings from Jacob's descendants. Also, God promises the land to Jacob that He promised to Abraham and Isaac.

Reuben has sex with Bilhah. This is not appropriate behavior. In today's society, it would be like a man sleeping with his stepmother. Although there is no commentary on this action at this time, Jacob mentions this action when he blesses his sons in Genesis 49.

Jacob experiences the death of two significant people—his wife, whom he loves, dies during childbirth. Rachel initially names their son because of her suffering, but Jacob renames him, signifying a place of favor. Jacob's father, Isaac, also dies. Now Jacob and his descendants are the bearers of the covenant that God made to Abraham.

The chapter ends with a list of the sons of Jacob because now the focus for the remaining chapters of Genesis is going to be the sons of Jacob.

Review
1. Discuss Genesis 35:1–7 and the commitment Jacob makes to the Lord.
2. Compare and contrast Genesis 35:9–15 to Genesis 17:4–9.
3. What name does Rachel give her second son, and what name does Israel give him?
4. What sinful act does Reuben commit?
5. List all the sons of Jacob and their mothers' names.

Genesis Chapter 36

1 Now these are the generations of Esau, who is Edom.

2 Esau took his wives of the daughters of Canaan; Adah the daughter of Elon the Hittite, and Aholibamah the daughter of Anah the daughter of Zibeon the Hivite;

3 And Bashemath Ishmael's daughter, sister of Nebajoth.

4 And Adah bare to Esau Eliphaz; and Bashemath bare Reuel;

5 And Aholibamah bare Jeush, and Jaalam, and Korah: these are the sons of Esau, which were born unto him in the land of Canaan.

6 And Esau took his wives, and his sons, and his daughters, and all the persons of his house, and his cattle, and all his beasts, and all his substance, which he had got in the land of Canaan; and went into the country from the face of his brother Jacob.

7 For their riches were more than that they might dwell together; and the land wherein they were strangers could not bear them because of their cattle.

8 Thus dwelt Esau in mount Seir: Esau is Edom.

9 And these are the generations of Esau the father of the Edomites in mount Seir:

10 These are the names of Esau's sons; Eliphaz the son of Adah the wife of Esau, Reuel the son of Bashemath the wife of Esau.

11 And the sons of Eliphaz were Teman, Omar, Zepho, and Gatam, and Kenaz.

12 And Timna was concubine to Eliphaz Esau's son; and she bare to Eliphaz Amalek: these were the sons of Adah Esau's wife.

13 And these are the sons of Reuel; Nahath, and Zerah, Shammah, and Mizzah: these were the sons of Bashemath Esau's wife.

14 And these were the sons of Aholibamah, the daughter of Anah the daughter of Zibeon, Esau's wife: and she bare to Esau Jeush, and Jaalam, and Korah.

15 These were dukes of the sons of Esau: the sons of Eliphaz the firstborn son of Esau; duke Teman, duke Omar, duke Zepho, duke Kenaz,

16 Duke Korah, duke Gatam, and duke Amalek: these are the dukes that came of Eliphaz in the land of Edom; these were the sons of Adah.

17 And these are the sons of Reuel Esau's son; duke Nahath, duke Zerah, duke Shammah, duke Mizzah: these are the dukes that came of Reuel in the land of Edom; these are the sons of Bashemath Esau's wife.

18 And these are the sons of Aholibamah Esau's wife; duke Jeush, duke Jaalam, duke Korah: these were the dukes that came of Aholibamah the daughter of Anah, Esau's wife.

19 These are the sons of Esau, who is Edom, and these are their dukes.

20 These are the sons of Seir the Horite, who inhabited the land; Lotan, and Shobal, and Zibeon, and Anah,

21 And Dishon, and Ezer, and Dishan: these are the dukes of the Horites, the children of Seir in the land of Edom.

22 And the children of Lotan were Hori and Hemam; and Lotan's sister was Timna.

23 And the children of Shobal were these; Alvan, and Manahath, and Ebal, Shepho, and Onam.

24 And these are the children of Zibeon; both Ajah, and Anah: this was that Anah that found the mules in the wilderness, as he fed the asses of Zibeon his father.

25 And the children of Anah were these; Dishon, and Aholibamah the daughter of Anah.

26 And these are the children of Dishon; Hemdan, and Eshban, and Ithran, and Cheran.

27 The children of Ezer are these; Bilhan, and Zaavan, and Akan.

28 The children of Dishan are these; Uz, and Aran.

29 These are the dukes that came of the Horites; duke Lotan, duke Shobal, duke Zibeon, duke Anah,

30 Duke Dishon, duke Ezer, duke Dishan: these are the dukes that came of Hori, among their dukes in the land of Seir.

31 And these are the kings that reigned in the land of Edom, before there reigned any king over the children of Israel.

32 And Bela the son of Beor reigned in Edom: and the name of his city was Dinhabah.

33 And Bela died, and Jobab the son of Zerah of Bozrah reigned in his stead.

34 And Jobab died, and Husham of the land of Temani reigned in his stead.

35 And Husham died, and Hadad the son of Bedad, who smote Midian in the field of Moab, reigned in his stead: and the name of his city was Avith.

36 And Hadad died, and Samlah of Masrekah reigned in his stead.

37 And Samlah died, and Saul of Rehoboth by the river reigned in his stead.

38 And Saul died, and Baal-hanan the son of Achbor reigned in his stead.

39 And Baal-hanan the son of Achbor died, and Hadar reigned in his stead: and the name of his city was Pau; and his wife's name was Mehetabel, the daughter of Matred, the daughter of Mezahab.

40 And these are the names of the dukes that came of Esau, according to their families, after their places, by their names; duke Timnah, duke Allah, duke Jetheth,

41 Duke Aholibamah, duke Elah, duke Pinon,

42 Duke Kenaz, duke Teman, duke Mibzar,

43 Duke Magdiel, duke Iram: these be the dukes of Edom, according to their habitations in the land of their possession: he is Esau the father of the Edomites.

Summary/Commentary

This chapter presents the descendants of Esau. Esau is Edom and the father of the Edomites. *Edom* means "red." Esau settles in Mount Seir. The text is clear that Esau and Jacob have to separate because they both have too many cattle to dwell together. This is similar to Abraham and Lot. In verse 20, there is a list of the descendants of Seir the Horite who lived in the land. There is also a list of the kings of Edom. The author stresses that Edom was ruled by kings before the Israelites have a king. In verse 12, we see the birth of Amalek, who becomes the father of the Amalekites. This is significant to the Israelites because they encounter the Edomites and Amalekites throughout their history.

Review
1. Who is the father of the nation of Edom?
2. Why can't Jacob and Esau dwell together in the same land?
3. Which nation has kings first, Israel or Edom?
4. Who are the Amalekites?
5. List at least one time the Israelites encounter the Edomites.

Genesis Chapter 37

1 *And Jacob dwelt in the land wherein his father was a stranger, in the land of Canaan.*

2 These are the generations of Jacob. Joseph, being seventeen years old, was feeding the flock with his brethren; and the lad was with the sons of Bilhah, and with the sons of Zilpah, his father's wives: and Joseph brought unto his father their evil report.

3 Now Israel loved Joseph more than all his children, because he was the son of his old age: and he made him a coat of many colours.

4 And when his brethren saw that their father loved him more than all his brethren, they hated him, and could not speak peaceably unto him.

5 And Joseph dreamed a dream, and he told it his brethren: and they hated him yet the more.

6 And he said unto them, Hear, I pray you, this dream which I have dreamed:

7 For, behold, we were binding sheaves in the field, and, lo, my sheaf arose, and also stood upright; and, behold, your sheaves stood round about, and made obeisance to my sheaf.

8 And his brethren said to him, Shalt thou indeed reign over us? or shalt thou indeed have dominion over us? And they hated him yet the more for his dreams, and for his words.

9 And he dreamed yet another dream, and told it his brethren, and said, Behold, I have dreamed a dream more; and, behold, the sun and the moon and the eleven stars made obeisance to me.

10 And he told it to his father, and to his brethren: and his father rebuked him, and said unto him, What is this dream that thou hast dreamed? Shall I and thy mother and thy brethren indeed come to bow down ourselves to thee to the earth?

11 And his brethren envied him; but his father observed the saying.

12 And his brethren went to feed their father's flock in Shechem.

13 And Israel said unto Joseph, Do not thy brethren feed the flock in Shechem? come, and I will send thee unto them. And he said to him, Here am I.

14 And he said to him, Go, I pray thee, see whether it be well with thy brethren, and well with the flocks; and bring me word again. So he sent him out of the vale of Hebron, and he came to Shechem.

15 And a certain man found him, and, behold, he was wandering in the field: and the man asked him, saying, What seekest thou?

16 And he said, I seek my brethren: tell me, I pray thee, where they feed their flocks.

17 And the man said, They are departed hence; for I heard them say, Let us go to Dothan. And Joseph went after his brethren, and found them in Dothan.

18 And when they saw him afar off, even before he came near unto them, they conspired against him to slay him.

19 And they said one to another, Behold, this dreamer cometh.

20 Come now therefore, and let us slay him, and cast him into some pit, and we will say, Some evil beast hath devoured him: and we shall see what will become of his dreams.

21 And Reuben heard it, and he delivered him out of their hands; and said, Let us not kill him.

22 And Reuben said unto them, Shed no blood, but cast him into this pit that is in the wilderness, and lay no hand upon him; that he might rid him out of their hands, to deliver him to his father again.

23 And it came to pass, when Joseph was come unto his brethren, that they stript Joseph out of his coat, his coat of many colours that was on him;

24 And they took him, and cast him into a pit: and the pit was empty, there was no water in it.

25 And they sat down to eat bread: and they lifted up their eyes and looked, and, behold, a company of Ishmeelites came from Gilead, with their camels bearing spicery and balm and myrrh, going to carry it down to Egypt.

26 And Judah said unto his brethren, What profit is it if we slay our brother, and conceal his blood?

27 Come, and let us sell him to the Ishmeelites, and let not our hand be upon him; for he is our brother and our flesh. And his brethren were content.

28 Then there passed by Midianites merchantmen; and they drew and lifted up Joseph out of the pit, and sold Joseph to the Ishmeelites for twenty pieces of silver: and they brought Joseph into Egypt.

29 And Reuben returned unto the pit; and, behold, Joseph was not in the pit; and he rent his clothes.

30 And he returned unto his brethren, and said, The child is not; and I, whither shall I go?

31 And they took Joseph's coat, and killed a kid of the goats, and dipped the coat in the blood;

32 And they sent the coat of many colours, and they brought it to their father; and said, This have we found: know now whether it be thy son's coat or no.

33 And he knew it, and said, It is my son's coat; an evil beast hath devoured him; Joseph is without doubt rent in pieces.

34 And Jacob rent his clothes, and put sackcloth upon his loins, and mourned for his son many days.

35 And all his sons and all his daughters rose up to comfort him; but he refused to be comforted; and he said, For I will go down into the grave unto my son mourning. Thus his father wept for him.

36 And the Midianites sold him into Egypt unto Potiphar, an officer of Pharaoh's, and captain of the guard.

Summary

vv. 1–2

Jacob lives in the land of Canaan. This is now the story of Jacob's descendants. Joseph is seventeen years old. Joseph is feeding the flock with his brothers whose mothers are Bilhah and Zilpah (Dan, Naphtali, Gad, and Asher) and comes back with a negative report about them.

vv. 3–4

Israel loves Joseph more than his brothers because Jacob was older when Joseph was born, and Jacob makes him a nice coat. When Joseph's brothers realize that their father favors Joseph, they hate him and can't say anything nice to him.

vv. 5–11

Joseph has a dream, and when he tells his brothers about it, they hate him even more. Joseph describes his dream. In it, he and his brothers are binding sheaves in the field, and all his brother's sheaves bow to his. His brothers respond by asking if Joseph is going to reign over them. Joseph has a second dream where the sun, the moon, and the eleven stars bow to him. This time, he tells his father and his brothers. His father rebukes Joseph and asks if he and his mother are going to bow down to him. His brothers resent him even more, but his father wonders about the meaning of the dreams.

vv. 12–14
Joseph's brothers go out to feed their father's sheep. Israel sends Joseph to check on his brothers and report back to him.

vv. 15–17
Joseph goes to Shechem looking for his brothers, but they aren't there. A stranger tells him that they have gone to Dothan, so Joseph travels there.

vv. 18–22
Joseph's brothers see him coming and start plotting against him. They mock him by calling him a dreamer. They first want to kill him and put him into a pit and say some beast ate him. Reuben tells his brothers not to kill Joseph but just to leave him in the pit. Reuben plans to come back later and get Joseph out and bring him back to their father.

vv. 23–24
When Joseph arrives, his brothers take his coat and throw him into an empty pit.

vv. 25–28
Joseph's brothers sit and eat. When some Ishmaelites are passing by, Judah thinks it would be better to sell Joseph and make a profit than to kill him. The brothers agree to sell him to the Ishmaelites instead of killing him. After all, Joseph is their brother, their own flesh. The Midianites lift Joseph out of the pit, and the brothers sell Joseph for twenty pieces of silver. The Ishmaelites take Joseph to Egypt.

vv. 29–36
Reuben returns and is disappointed when he finds the pit empty. The brothers take Joseph's coat and put blood on it and tell their father a beast killed Joseph. Jacob mourns Joseph's death, and all his children try to comfort him, but he says he will mourn Joseph until he dies. The Midianites sell Joseph to Potiphar, the captain of the guard in Egypt.

Commentary

Now the narrative has shifted from Jacob to his sons and to one son specifically, Joseph. We know Joseph's age, which means he is significantly younger than his brothers. We also know that Joseph is Jacob's favorite and Jacob makes this obvious by giving Joseph a special gift. There is a lot of animosity in this family. Not only is Joseph the favorite, but Joseph also gives his father a negative report about his brothers. There is so much jealousy and hatred toward Joseph that his brothers consider killing him. (This is another example of brothers desiring to kill a brother, like Cain and Abel. Then Esau desires to kill Jacob, and now Joseph's brothers desired to kill him.) Reuben convinces his brothers not to kill Joseph but to throw him into an empty pit. As the oldest, the brothers will still follow Reuben's direction. Reuben is going to save Joseph and present him to Jacob, possibly trying to gain favor with Jacob. While Reuben is gone, his brothers decide to sell Joseph instead of killing him. It is interesting that when the brothers decide to sell Joseph, they focus on Joseph being their own flesh. It appears that they have some guilt about the idea of harming him.

Dreams play a significant role in the Joseph narrative. As Joseph transitions from favorite son, to slave, to prisoner, and to governor, dreams are significant throughout Joseph's life. Joseph has two dreams that are a foreshadowing of the future. The first one describes his brother's sheaves bowing to him, and the second describes the sun, moon, and eleven stars bowing to him. Jacob and his sons understand that these dreams mean that Joseph will have authority over them. Neither Jacob nor his sons think this will happen and speak negatively toward Joseph because of his dreams.

In the text, it seems the brothers sell Joseph to both the Ishmaelites and to Midianites. Some people suggest that these are just generic terms for wandering tribes.[76]

Reuben and Jacob both express sorrow for the loss of Joseph. The terms "rent his clothes" and "put on a sackcloth" describe signs of mourning.[77]

Review
1. Why do Joseph's brothers dislike him? Is Joseph aware of this?
2. Describe Joseph's two dreams.
3. What does Reuben plan to do with Joseph?
4. What do Joseph's brothers do with him before Reuben returns?
5. Who are the Ishmaelites and Midianites?

---

[76] Walton, *Genesis*, 665.
[77] Wenham, *Word Biblical Commentary*, 2:356.

Genesis Chapter 38

1 *And it came to pass at that time, that Judah went down from his brethren, and turned in to a certain Adullamite, whose name was Hirah.*

2 And Judah saw there a daughter of a certain Canaanite, whose name was Shuah; and he took her, and went in unto her.

3 And she conceived, and bare a son; and he called his name Er.

4 And she conceived again, and bare a son; and she called his name Onan.

5 And she yet again conceived, and bare a son; and called his name Shelah: and he was at Chezib, when she bare him.

6 And Judah took a wife for Er his firstborn, whose name was Tamar.

7 And Er, Judah's firstborn, was wicked in the sight of the LORD; and the LORD slew him.

8 And Judah said unto Onan, Go in unto thy brother's wife, and marry her, and raise up seed to thy brother.

9 And Onan knew that the seed should not be his; and it came to pass, when he went in unto his brother's wife, that he spilled it on the ground, lest that he should give seed to his brother.

10 And the thing which he did displeased the LORD: wherefore he slew him also.

11 Then said Judah to Tamar his daughter in law, Remain a widow at thy father's house, till Shelah my son be grown: for he said, Lest peradventure he die also, as his brethren did. And Tamar went and dwelt in her father's house.

12 And in process of time the daughter of Shuah Judah's wife died; and Judah was comforted, and went up unto his sheepshearers to Timnath, he and his friend Hirah the Adullamite.

13 And it was told Tamar, saying, Behold thy father in law goeth up to Timnath to shear his sheep.

14 And she put her widow's garments off from her, and covered her with a vail, and wrapped herself, and sat in an open place, which is by the way to Timnath; for she saw that Shelah was grown, and she was not given unto him to wife.

15 When Judah saw her, he thought her to be an harlot; because she had covered her face.

16 And he turned unto her by the way, and said, Go to, I pray thee, let me come in unto thee; (for he knew not that she was his daughter in law.) And she said, What wilt thou give me, that thou mayest come in unto me?

17 And he said, I will send thee a kid from the flock. And she said, Wilt thou give me a pledge, till thou send it?

18 And he said, What pledge shall I give thee? And she said, Thy signet, and thy bracelets, and thy staff that is in thine hand. And he gave it her, and came in unto her, and she conceived by him.

19 And she arose, and went away, and laid by her vail from her, and put on the garments of her widowhood.

20 And Judah sent the kid by the hand of his friend the Adullamite, to receive his pledge from the woman's hand: but he found her not.

21 Then he asked the men of that place, saying, Where is the harlot, that was openly by the way side? And they said, There was no harlot in this place.

22 And he returned to Judah, and said, I cannot find her; and also the men of the place said, that there was no harlot in this place.

23 And Judah said, Let her take it to her, lest we be shamed: behold, I sent this kid, and thou hast not found her.

24 And it came to pass about three months after, that it was told Judah, saying, Tamar thy daughter in law hath played the harlot; and also, behold, she is with child by whoredom. And Judah said, Bring her forth, and let her be burnt.

25 When she was brought forth, she sent to her father in law, saying, By the man, whose these are, am I with child: and she said, Discern, I pray thee, whose are these, the signet, and bracelets, and staff.

26 And Judah acknowledged them, and said, She hath been more righteous than I; because that I gave her not to Shelah my son. And he knew her again no more.

27 And it came to pass in the time of her travail, that, behold, twins were in her womb.

28 And it came to pass, when she travailed, that the one put out his hand: and the midwife took and bound upon his hand a scarlet thread, saying, This came out first.

29 And it came to pass, as he drew back his hand, that, behold, his brother came out: and she said, How hast thou broken forth? this breach be upon thee: therefore his name was called Pharez.

30 And afterward came out his brother, that had the scarlet thread upon his hand: and his name was called Zarah.

Summary

vv. 1–5

Judah travels away from his brothers, moves to Adullam, and stays with a man named Hirah. He marries a Canaanite woman whose father is Shuah. They have three sons named Er, Onan, and Shelah.

vv. 6–11

Judah finds a wife for Er, and her name is Tamar. Er is wicked, so God kills him. Judah instructs Onan to marry Tamar and raise children in his brother's name.[78] Onan spills his seed because he knows the children will not be considered his children. Onan spilling his seed is not pleasing to the Lord, so God kills him also. Judah instructs Tamar to stay at her father's house and keep herself as a widow, and when his youngest son is of age, Judah will give Shelah to her as her husband. But Judah has no intentions of fulfilling this obligation because he is afraid his youngest son will die also.

vv. 12–18

Judah's wife dies, and he goes to shear sheep in Timnath with Hirah the Adullamite. Tamar is told that Judah is going to Timnath to shear sheep. Tamar removes her widow garments and covers herself with a veil and sits in a place where she can be seen on the way to Timnath. Shelah is now old enough to be married, but Judah does not keep his promise to give him to Tamar for a husband. Judah sees Tamar and propositions her. He states he will send her a goat. She asks for collateral until she receives the goat, and Judah gives her his signet, bracelets, and staff. They have sexual relations, and she conceives.

vv. 19–26

Tamar puts back on her widow's clothes. Judah sends the goat as payment with the Adullamite, but he cannot find her. He asks the men in the area, and they

---

[78] Walton, *Genesis*, 667–668.

say there is no harlot in this area. He returns and tells Judah that he cannot find her, and Judah states she can have his things because he will be embarrassed if he continues to look for her. Three months later, Judah is told that Tamar acted like a harlot and is pregnant. Judah orders her to come to him, and she is to be burned as punishment. When Tamar comes before Judah, she tells him that she is pregnant by the man who owns the signet, bracelets, and staff. At this point, Judah acknowledges that he was in the wrong by not giving Shelah to her as a husband, and Judah never has sexual relations with her again.

vv. 27–30
Tamar has twins. The oldest is Pharez, and the youngest is Zerah.

Commentary
This chapter seems as if it is an outlier because it describes the life of Judah instead of continuing with the story of Joseph. Although Joseph is the significant son of Jacob in that it is through him that his family is saved, Judah is also significant to the Israelite people. The original audience would have been interested in Judah's story. It is the line of Pharez that produces King David and Jesus Christ.

It appears that Judah faults Tamar for his sons' deaths. In reality, Judah marries a Canaanite woman, which God does not approve of, and both his sons do something that God is displeased with. It does not seem to occur to Judah that he and his sons might be responsible for their deaths.

There is no such thing as a perfect family, except maybe on television sitcoms. Many people view themselves negatively because their families are not perfect. Some people even feel that God does not love them or they are not worthy of His love because of how they were raised. Judah has sex with his daughter-in-law, whom he thinks is a prostitute, and produces the son who is the ancestor of Jesus. This passage informs us that even in the lineage of Jesus, there is family dysfunction.

Review
1. Who is Judah?
2. Why is Tamar to remain a widow at her father's house?
3. How does Tamar disguise herself from Judah?
4. How does Judah discover his inappropriate behavior toward Tamar?
5. Who are Pharez and Zarah, and how are they related to Jesus?

Genesis Chapter 39

1 *And Joseph was brought down to Egypt; and Potiphar, an officer of Pharaoh, captain of the guard, an Egyptian, bought him of the hands of the Ishmeelites, which had brought him down thither.*

2 And the LORD was with Joseph, and he was a prosperous man; and he was in the house of his master the Egyptian.

3 And his master saw that the LORD was with him, and that the LORD made all that he did to prosper in his hand.

4 And Joseph found grace in his sight, and he served him: and he made him overseer over his house, and all that he had he put into his hand.

5 And it came to pass from the time that he had made him overseer in his house, and over all that he had, that the LORD blessed the Egyptian's house for Joseph's sake; and the blessing of the LORD was upon all that he had in the house, and in the field.

6 And he left all that he had in Joseph's hand; and he knew not ought he had, save the bread which he did eat. And Joseph was a goodly person, and well favoured.

7 And it came to pass after these things, that his master's wife cast her eyes upon Joseph; and she said, Lie with me.

8 But he refused, and said unto his master's wife, Behold, my master wotteth not what is with me in the house, and he hath committed all that he hath to my hand;

9 There is none greater in this house than I; neither hath he kept back any thing from me but thee, because thou art his wife: how then can I do this great wickedness, and sin against God?

10 And it came to pass, as she spake to Joseph day by day, that he hearkened not unto her, to lie by her, or to be with her.

11 And it came to pass about this time, that Joseph went into the house to do his business; and there was none of the men of the house there within.

12 And she caught him by his garment, saying, Lie with me: and he left his garment in her hand, and fled, and got him out.

13 And it came to pass, when she saw that he had left his garment in her hand, and was fled forth,

14 That she called unto the men of her house, and spake unto them, saying, See, he hath brought in an Hebrew unto us to mock us; he came in unto me to lie with me, and I cried with a loud voice:

15 And it came to pass, when he heard that I lifted up my voice and cried, that he left his garment with me, and fled, and got him out.

16 And she laid up his garment by her, until his lord came home.

17 And she spake unto him according to these words, saying, The Hebrew servant, which thou hast brought unto us, came in unto me to mock me:

18 And it came to pass, as I lifted up my voice and cried, that he left his garment with me, and fled out.

19 And it came to pass, when his master heard the words of his wife, which she spake unto him, saying, After this manner did thy servant to me; that his wrath was kindled.

20 And Joseph's master took him, and put him into the prison, a place where the king's prisoners were bound: and he was there in the prison.

21 But the LORD was with Joseph, and shewed him mercy, and gave him favour in the sight of the keeper of the prison.

22 And the keeper of the prison committed to Joseph's hand all the prisoners that were in the prison; and whatsoever they did there, he was the doer of it.

23 The keeper of the prison looked not to any thing that was under his hand; because the LORD was with him, and that which he did, the LORD made it to prosper.

Summary
vv. 1–6

Potiphar, who is an officer of Pharaoh in Egypt, buys Joseph from the Ishmaelites. God is with Joseph, and he prospers in Potiphar's house. Potiphar sees that the Lord is with Joseph and that the Lord blesses everything Joseph does. Joseph finds favor with Potiphar, and he sets Joseph over everything in his house.

After Potiphar appoints Joseph as overseer of his house, the Lord blesses Potiphar's house and his land. Potiphar leaves everything up to Joseph. The only thing Potiphar thinks about is what food he wants to eat. Joseph is an attractive young man.

vv. 7–20

Potiphar's wife propositions Joseph, but he refuses. He states that Potiphar has withheld nothing back from him but his wife. Joseph says that he cannot sin against God. Potiphar's wife continues to proposition Joseph every day, but he does not agree to have sex with her. One day Joseph goes into the house to do his regular duties, and there is no one else in the house except Potiphar's wife. She grabs him by his coat and asks him to have sex with her, and Joseph runs out, but she realizes he has left his coat behind. So she calls the male servants and lies, saying that Joseph tried to have sex with her, and she presents his coat as proof. She retells the same story to Potiphar, and he becomes angry and throws Joseph into prison.

vv. 21–23

God is still with Joseph in prison, and he has favor with the warden. The warden puts Joseph in charge of the other prisoners. The warden does not worry about anything because the Lord is with Joseph and causes everything that Joseph does to prosper.

Commentary

This chapter continues Joseph's narrative. Although Joseph is a slave in a foreign land, we see that God continues to bless him. A common statement throughout the Joseph narrative is "the Lord was with Joseph." Although Joseph experiences several horrendous circumstances, the author continues to remind us that Joseph has the favor of God. The Joseph narrative is different from the narratives of Abraham, Isaac, and Jacob. There is no record that Joseph has the same type of personal encounter that the patriarchs experienced. Although Joseph is the "covenant" bearer of his generation, he does not experience having God talk to him and directly blessing him as the patriarchs have.

From this incident with Potiphar's wife, one can see that Joseph is a man of good character. He states that he will not sin against God. This is in contrast to his brothers Rueben, who slept with his father's handmaid, and Judah, who slept with his daughter-in-law. Although Joseph does what was right, he is still punished. This is an excellent example of godly character because Joseph does what is right despite tempting circumstances.

Also, we can tell that this book was written by Moses when the Israelites were a nation because Joseph is referenced as a Hebrew in verse 14, and at that time, there was no Hebrew nation.

Review
1. What is Joseph's position in Potiphar's house?
2. What does it mean in Genesis 39:6 where it states, "Joseph was a goodly person and well favored."?
3. What does Joseph's response in Genesis 39:8 say about his character?
4. How does Joseph end up in jail?
5. How does the keeper of the prison feel toward Joseph?

Genesis Chapter 40

1 *And it came to pass after these things, that the butler of the king of Egypt and his baker had offended their lord the king of Egypt.*

2 And Pharaoh was wroth against two of his officers, against the chief of the butlers, and against the chief of the bakers.

3 And he put them in ward in the house of the captain of the guard, into the prison, the place where Joseph was bound.

4 And the captain of the guard charged Joseph with them, and he served them: and they continued a season in ward.

5 And they dreamed a dream both of them, each man his dream in one night, each man according to the interpretation of his dream, the butler and the baker of the king of Egypt, which were bound in the prison.

6 And Joseph came in unto them in the morning, and looked upon them, and, behold, they were sad.

7 And he asked Pharaoh's officers that were with him in the ward of his lord's house, saying, Wherefore look ye so sadly to day?

8 And they said unto him, We have dreamed a dream, and there is no interpreter of it. And Joseph said unto them, Do not interpretations belong to God? tell me them, I pray you.

9 And the chief butler told his dream to Joseph, and said to him, In my dream, behold, a vine was before me;

10 And in the vine were three branches: and it was as though it budded, and her blossoms shot forth; and the clusters thereof brought forth ripe grapes:

11 And Pharaoh's cup was in my hand: and I took the grapes, and pressed them into Pharaoh's cup, and I gave the cup into Pharaoh's hand.

12 And Joseph said unto him, This is the interpretation of it: The three branches are three days:

13 Yet within three days shall Pharaoh lift up thine head, and restore thee unto thy place: and thou shalt deliver Pharaoh's cup into his hand, after the former manner when thou wast his butler.

14 But think on me when it shall be well with thee, and shew kindness, I pray thee, unto me, and make mention of me unto Pharaoh, and bring me out of this house:

15 For indeed I was stolen away out of the land of the Hebrews: and here also have I done nothing that they should put me into the dungeon.

16 When the chief baker saw that the interpretation was good, he said unto Joseph, I also was in my dream, and, behold, I had three white baskets on my head:

17 And in the uppermost basket there was of all manner of bake meats for Pharaoh; and the birds did eat them out of the basket upon my head.

18 And Joseph answered and said, This is the interpretation thereof: The three baskets are three days:

19 Yet within three days shall Pharaoh lift up thy head from off thee, and shall hang thee on a tree; and the birds shall eat thy flesh from off thee.

20 And it came to pass the third day, which was Pharaoh's birthday, that he made a feast unto all his servants: and he lifted up the head of the chief butler and of the chief baker among his servants.

21 And he restored the chief butler unto his butlership again; and he gave the cup into Pharaoh's hand:

22 But he hanged the chief baker: as Joseph had interpreted to them.

23 Yet did not the chief butler remember Joseph, but forgat him.

Summary
vv. 1–4
The chief butler and chief baker to Pharaoh offend him and are placed in the same prison that Joseph is in. The head of the prison places Joseph in charge of them.

vv. 5–8
They both have dreams and appear troubled, so Joseph asks them what is wrong. They answer by stating that they've had dreams but have no one to interpret them. Joseph says that dream interpretation belongs to God and asks them to tell him their dreams.

vv. 9–15

The butler tells Joseph his dream first. In the butler's dream, there are three vine branches that begin to bud, blossom, and produce grapes. He is holding Pharaoh's wine glass in his hand. The butler squeezes the juice from the grapes into the glass and gives it to Pharaoh. Joseph interprets the dream. He states that the three vines represent three days, and in three days, the Pharaoh will restore the butler to his position. Joseph asks the butler to remember him when Pharaoh restores him to his position because he has been stolen from his home and has done nothing to deserve being placed in prison.

vv. 16–18

When the baker hears that the butler's dream has a positive result, he tells Joseph his dream. In the baker's dream, there are three baskets filled with pastries on his head for Pharaoh. Birds come and eat them off the head of the baker. Joseph tells the baker that the three baskets represent three days. In three days, the Pharaoh will hang the baker, and the birds will eat his flesh.

vv. 19–23

In three days, it is Pharaoh's birthday, and he has a big celebration. Just as Joseph has said, he restores the butler and hangs the baker. Unfortunately, the butler does not remember Joseph.

Commentary

Although many people today believe that dreams have meaning, dreams during Joseph's time had an even greater significance. It was believed that dreams were future prophecies or that they were God talking to the dreamers. Joseph is able to interpret the dreams of the butler and the baker, but he gives the credit to God. Joseph's ability to interpret dreams is significant to his narrative. Unfortunately, when the butler is restored, he does not remember Joseph. This is one of the few times in Joseph's narrative that he makes any complaint when he states that he has been taken from his homeland and has been unjustly placed in prison. At this point, it seems that despite Joseph's favor with God, he may be stuck in prison.

Review

1. Why do the chief baker and butler go to prison?
2. What does Joseph mean in Genesis 40:8 when he says," Do not interpretations belong to God?"
3. Describe the butler's dream and its interpretation.

4. Describe the baker's dream and its interpretation.
5. Does the butler remember Joseph as he promised?

Genesis Chapter 41

1   *And it came to pass at the end of two full years, that Pharaoh dreamed: and, behold, he stood by the river.*

2 And, behold, there came up out of the river seven well favoured kine and fatfleshed; and they fed in a meadow.

3 And, behold, seven other kine came up after them out of the river, ill favoured and leanfleshed; and stood by the other kine upon the brink of the river.

4 And the ill favoured and leanfleshed kine did eat up the seven well favoured and fat kine. So Pharaoh awoke.

5 And he slept and dreamed the second time: and, behold, seven ears of corn came up upon one stalk, rank and good.

6 And, behold, seven thin ears and blasted with the east wind sprung up after them.

7 And the seven thin ears devoured the seven rank and full ears. And Pharaoh awoke, and, behold, it was a dream.

8 And it came to pass in the morning that his spirit was troubled; and he sent and called for all the magicians of Egypt, and all the wise men thereof: and Pharaoh told them his dream; but there was none that could interpret them unto Pharaoh.

9 Then spake the chief butler unto Pharaoh, saying, I do remember my faults this day:

10 Pharaoh was wroth with his servants, and put me in ward in the captain of the guard's house, both me and the chief baker:

11 And we dreamed a dream in one night, I and he; we dreamed each man according to the interpretation of his dream.

12 And there was there with us a young man, and Hebrew, servant to the captain of the guard; and we told him, and he interpreted to us our dreams; to each man according to his dream he did interpret.

13 And it came to pass, as he interpreted to us, so it was; me he restored unto mine office, and him he hanged.

14 Then Pharaoh sent and called Joseph, and they brought him hastily out of the dungeon: and he shaved himself, and changed his raiment, and came in unto Pharaoh.

15 And Pharaoh said unto Joseph, I have dreamed a dream, and there is none that can interpret it: and I have heard say of thee, that thou canst understand a dream to interpret it.

16 And Joseph answered Pharaoh, saying, It is not in me: God shall give Pharaoh an answer of peace.

17 And Pharaoh said unto Joseph, In my dream, behold, I stood upon the bank of the river:

18 And, behold, there came up out of the river seven kine, fatfleshed and well favoured; and they fed in a meadow:

19 And, behold, seven other kine came up after them, poor and very ill favoured and leanfleshed, such as I never saw in all the land of Egypt for badness:

20 And the lean and the ill favoured kine did eat up the first seven fat kine:

21 And when they had eaten them up, it could not be known that they had eaten them; but they were still ill favoured, as at the beginning. So I awoke.

22 And I saw in my dream, and, behold, seven ears came up in one stalk, full and good:

23 And, behold, seven ears, withered, thin, and blasted with the east wind, sprung up after them:

24 And the thin ears devoured the seven good ears: and I told this unto the magicians; but there was none that could declare it to me.

25 And Joseph said unto Pharaoh, The dream of Pharaoh is one God hath shewed Pharaoh what he is about to do.

26 The seven good kine are seven years; and the seven good ears are seven years: the dream is one.

27 And the seven thin and ill favoured kine that came up after them are seven years; and the seven empty ears blasted with the eastward shall be seven years of famine.

28 This is the thing which I have spoken unto Pharaoh: What God is about to do he sheweth unto Pharaoh.

29 Behold, there come seven years of great plenty throughout all the land of Egypt.

30 And there shall arise after them seven years of famine; and all the plenty shall be forgotten in the land of Egypt; and the famine shall consume the land;

31 And the plenty shall not be known in the land by reason of that famine following; for it shall be very grievous.

32 And for that the dream was doubled unto Pharaoh twice; it is because the thing is established by God, and God will shortly bring it to pass.

33 Now therefore let Pharaoh look out a man discreet and wise, and set him over the land of Egypt.

34 Let Pharaoh do this, and let him appoint officers over the land, and take up the fifth part of the land of Egypt in the seven plenteous years.

35 And let them gather all the food of those good years that come, and lay up corn under the hand of Pharaoh, and let them keep food in the cities.

36 And that food shall be for store to the land against the seven years of famine, which shall be in the land of Egypt; that the land perish not through the famine.

37 And the thing was good in the eyes of Pharaoh, and in the yes of all his servants.

38 And Pharaoh said unto his servants, Can we find such a one as this is, a man in whom the Spirit of God is?

39 And Pharaoh said unto Joseph, Forasmuch as God hath shewed thee all this, there is none so discreet and wise as thou art:

40 Thou shalt be over my house, and according unto thy word shall all my people be ruled: only in the throne will I be greater than thou.

41 And Pharaoh said unto Joseph, See I have set thee over all the land of Egypt.

42 And Pharaoh took off his ring from his hand, and put it upon Joseph's hand, and arrayed him in vestures of fine linen, and put a gold chain about his neck;

43 And he made him to ride in the second chariot which he had; and they cried before him, Bow the knee: and he made him ruler over all the land of Egypt.

44 And Pharaoh said unto Joseph, I am Pharaoh, and without thee shall no man lift up his hand or foot in all the land of Egypt.

45 And Pharaoh called Joseph's name Zaphnath-paaneah; and he gave him to wife Asenath the daughter of Poti-pherah priest of On. And Joseph went out over all the land of Egypt.

46 And Joseph was thirty years old when he stood before Pharaoh king of Egypt. And Joseph went out from the presence of Pharaoh, and went throughout all the land of Egypt.

47 And in the seven plenteous years the earth brought forth by handfuls.

48 And he gathered up all the food of the seven years, which were in the land of Egypt, and laid up the food in the cities: the food of the field, which was round about every city, laid he up in the same.

49 And Joseph gathered corners the sand of the sea, very much, until he left numbering; for it was without number.

50 And unto Joseph were born two sons before the years of famine, which Asenath the daughter of Poti-pherah priest of On bare unto him.

51 And Joseph called the name of the firstborn Manasseh: For God, said he hath made me forget all my toil, and all my father's house.

52 And the name of the second call he Ephraim: For God hath caused me to be fruitful in the land of my affliction.

53 And the seven years of plenteousness, that was in the land of Egypt, were ended.

54 And the seven years of dearth began to come, according as Joseph had said: and the dearth was in all lands; but in all the land of Egypt there was bread.

55 And when all the land of Egypt was famished, the people cried to Pharaoh for bread: and Pharaoh said unto all the Egyptians, Go unto Joseph; what he saith to you, do.

56 And the famine was over all the face of the earth: And Joseph opened all the storehouses, and sold unto the Egyptians; and the famine waxed sore in the land of Egypt.

57 And all countries came into Egypt to Joseph for to buy corn; because that the famine was so sore in all lands.

Summary

vv. 1–7

Two years later, Pharaoh has two dreams. He sees seven fat, healthy cows come out of the Nile followed by seven thin cows. The seven thin cows eat the seven fat cows. After this dream, he wakes up. He goes back to sleep and has another dream. In the second dream, Pharaoh sees seven good ears of corn growing on a cornstalk followed by seven scrawny ears growing on the same cornstalk. The seven scrawny ears of corn eat the seven good ears of corn. Then he wakes up again.

vv. 8–13

Pharaoh is troubled by the dreams and asks the magicians and wise men of Egypt to interpret them, but no one can. It is at this time that the butler finally remembers Joseph. The butler tells Pharaoh that while the butler had been in prison there was a Hebrew servant who correctly interpreted his dream and the baker's dream.

vv. 14–24

Pharaoh calls for Joseph, and Joseph is brought out of prison. Joseph shaves and changes his clothes before he goes before Pharaoh. Pharaoh tells Joseph that he has had a dream and that no one can interpret it. Joseph says it is God who will interpret Pharaoh's dream. Pharaoh recounts the details of his dream. Pharaoh states that he has told his dreams to all his magicians, and none of them can interpret them.

vv. 25–32

Joseph interprets Pharaoh's dreams. He states the two dreams are one and that God is showing Pharaoh what he is about to do. The seven fat, healthy cows are seven years, and the seven good ears of corn are seven years. The seven thin cows are seven years, and the seven scrawny ears of corn are seven years. The interpretation is that Egypt will have seven good years of plenty followed by seven years of famine. The famine will be so bad that everyone will forget the seven years of plenty. Pharaoh has had two dreams with the same interpretation because this is established by God, and He will bring it to pass very soon.

vv. 33–49

Joseph suggests to Pharaoh that he place someone in charge of storing food for the famine. Joseph recommends setting apart one-fifth of the harvest from the land during the time of plenty and storing the food to prepare for the time of famine. Pharaoh thinks that Joseph's idea is good. Pharaoh asks if he could find a better man than Joseph, who has the Spirit of God, to be placed in charge of organizing the food. Pharaoh states that God has shown Joseph this dream and that he is wise and discreet. Pharaoh places Joseph in charge of this process and states Joseph will be over all of Egypt. Only Pharaoh will be greater than Joseph. Pharaoh takes off his ring, puts it on Joseph's hand, gives him nice clothes, and puts a gold chain around his neck. Joseph rides in the second chariot, and the people bow toward him. Pharaoh calls Joseph *Zaphnath-paaneah*, meaning "the man to whom secrets are revealed," and gives him a wife, Asenath, who is the daughter of Poti-pherah, the priest of On. Joseph is thirty years old when this happens. The seven years of plenty come, and Joseph gathers up extra food and stores it throughout Egypt.

vv. 50–52

Joseph's sons, *Manasseh*, which means "forgetting," and *Ephraim*, which means "fruitful," are born.

vv. 53–57

The time of plenty ends, and the famine throughout the whole land begins, but there is food in Egypt. The Egyptians cry out to Pharaoh for food, and he tells them to follow Joseph's instructions. Joseph opens the storehouses and sells food to the people. People from other countries come to buy corn from Joseph because the famine is severe across the entire region.

Commentary

At the end of the last chapter, it seems as if Joseph is forgotten and is destined to stay in jail for something he did not do. Joseph is found to be faithful to God in the situation with Potiphar's wife. Joseph acknowledges God when he interprets dreams, and the text states that God is with Joseph. During these adverse situations, the Bible does not state that Joseph ever became discouraged or depressed.

When Pharaoh has the two dreams, Joseph is given the opportunity that he has hoped for, and he interprets Pharaoh's dreams. Pharaoh sees that Joseph has the Spirit of God and that he is blessed, so Pharaoh elevates Joseph to a high position. Now the land where Joseph was once a slave is the land in which he is a ruler. Not only has Joseph gained position and wealth, but he has also gained a wife and children. It takes thirteen years from when he was sold until he becomes the overseer of Egypt. He was seventeen when he was sold by his brothers and thirty when he interprets Pharaoh's dream. Even in these unjust circumstances that Joseph experiences, God is still faithful because He has now abundantly blessed Joseph. God is also still faithful to His covenant with Abraham because it is through Joseph that God is going to be able to provide food for Abraham's family.

Review

1. Describe Pharaoh's dream.
2. Who finally remembers Joseph?
3. What is Joseph's interpretation of Pharaoh's dream?
4. What position is Joseph given, and how does he plan to deal with the famine?
5. Name Joseph's sons and explain the meaning of their names.

Genesis Chapter 42

1 Now when Jacob saw that there was corn in Egypt, Jacob said unto his sons, Why do ye look one upon another?

2 And he said, Behold, I have heard that there is corn in Egypt: get you down thither, and buy for us from thence; that we may live, and not die.

3 And Joseph's ten brethren went down to buy corn in Egypt.

4 But Benjamin, Joseph's brother, Jacob sent not with his brethren; for he said, Lest peradventure mischief befall him.

5 And the sons of Israel came to buy corn among those that came: for the famine was in the land of Canaan.

6 And Joseph was the governor over the land, and he it was that sold to all the people of the land: and Joseph's brethren came, and bowed down themselves before him with their faces to the earth.

7 And Joseph saw his brethren, and he knew them, but made himself strange unto them, and spake roughly unto them; and he said unto them, Whence come ye? And they said, From the land of Canaan to buy food.

8 And Joseph knew his brethren, but they knew not him.

9 And Joseph remembered the dreams which he dreamed of them, and said unto them, Ye are spies; to see the nakedness of the land ye are come.

10 And they said unto him, Nay, my lord, but to buy food are thy servants come.

11 We are all one man's sons; we are true men, thy servants are no spies.

12 And he said unto them, Nay, but to see the nakedness of the land ye are come.

13 And they said, Thy servants are twelve brethren, the sons of one man in the land of Canaan; and, behold, the youngest is this day with our father, and one is not.

14 And Joseph said unto them, That is it that I spake unto you, saying, Ye are spies:

15 Hereby ye shall be proved: By the life of Pharaoh ye shall not go forth hence, except your youngest brother come hither.

16 Send one of you, and let him fetch your brother, and ye shall be kept in prison, that your words may be proved, whether there be any truth in you: or else by the life of Pharaoh surely ye are spies.

17 And he put them all together into ward three days

18 And Joseph said unto them the third day, This do, and live; for I fear God:

19 If ye be true men, let one of your brethren be bound in the house of your prison: go ye, carry corn for the famine of your houses:

20 But bring your youngest brother unto me; so shall your words be verified, and ye shall not die. And they did so.

21 And they said one to another, We are verily guilty concerning our brother, in that we saw the anguish of his soul, when he besought us, and we would not hear; therefore is this distress come upon us.

22 And Reuben answered them, saying, Spake I not unto you, saying, Do not sin against the child; and ye would not hear? therefore, behold, also his blood is required.

23 And they knew not that Joseph understood them; for he spake unto them by an interpreter.

24 And he turned himself about from them, and wept; and returned to them again, and communed with them, and took from them Simeon, and bound him before their eyes.

25 Then Joseph commanded to fill their sacks with corn, and to restore every man's money into his sack, and to give them provision for the way: and thus did he unto them.

26 And they laded their asses with the corn, and departed thence.

27 And as one of them opened his sack to give his ass provender in the inn, he espied his money; for, behold, it was in his sack's mouth.

28 And he said unto his brethren, My money is restored; and, lo, it is even in my sack: and their heart failed them, and they were afraid, saying one to another, What is this that God hath done unto us?

29 And they came unto Jacob their father unto the land of Canaan, and told him all that befell unto them saying,

30 The man, who is lord of the land, spake roughly to us, and took us for spies of the country.

31 And we said unto him, We are true men; we are no spies:

32 We be twelve brethren, sons of our father; one is not, and the youngest is this day with our father in the land of Canaan.

33 And the man, the lord of the country, said unto us, Hereby shall I know that ye are true men; leave one of your brethren here with me, and take food for the famine of your households, and be gone:

34 And bring your youngest brother unto me: then shall I know that ye are no spies, but that ye are true men: so will I deliver you your brother, and ye shall traffick in the land.

35 And it came to pass as they emptied their sacks, that, behold, every man's bundle of money was in his sack: and when both they and their father saw the bundles of money, they were afraid.

36 And Jacob their father said unto them, Me have ye bereaved of my children: Joseph is not, and Simeon is not, and ye will take Benjamin away: all these things are against me.

37 And Reuben spake unto his father, saying, Slay my two sons, if I bring him not to thee: deliver him into my hand, and I will bring him to thee again.

38 And he said, My son shall not go down with you; for his brother is dead, and he is left alone: if mischief befall him by the way in the which ye go, then shall ye bring down my gray hairs with sorrow to the grave.

Summary

vv. 1–5

Jacob knows that there is corn in Egypt and asks his sons to go buy corn. Jacob's ten sons go to Egypt to buy corn. Jacob will not send Benjamin, Joseph's full brother, because he does not want anything to happen to Benjamin. So Israel's sons go to Egypt to buy corn since the famine is severe in Canaan.

vv. 6–17

Joseph is the ruler of Egypt, and he sells corn to the people. His brothers come and bow to him. Joseph sees his brothers and hides his identity. He speaks harshly to them, asking them where they came from. They reply that they came from Canaan. Joseph recognizes them, but they do not recognize him. Joseph remembers his dreams and accuses them of being spies. They deny being spies and state they have only come to buy food. They state that they are one man's sons. They continue to say that their father has twelve sons, but the youngest is home with their father, and one is dead. Joseph still insists they are spies. Joseph gives them an opportunity to prove their innocence. He says one of them can go back home and bring the youngest brother while the rest will be in prison until they return. Joseph puts his brothers in prison for three days.

vv. 18–24
On the third day, Joseph gives them another opportunity to prove their innocence. Joseph suggests that one brother can stay in prison and the rest can leave and bring corn back to their family, but they must bring their youngest brother back for their older brother to be released. The brothers feel guilty for what they did to Joseph and believe that this is their punishment for selling him. Reuben says he told them not to hurt Joseph and that now they are guilty of his death. They do not know that Joseph understands what they are saying because he is using an interpreter. Joseph goes into another room to cry because he is overcome with emotion. When he returns, Joseph takes Simeon, binds him up, and keeps him as a prisoner.

vv. 25–28
Joseph commands his servants to fill his brother's sacks with corn, to return their money to them, and to give them supplies for their journey. On the journey back to Canaan, one brother discovers that the money they had given to the Egyptians for the food is still in his sack. Now they are afraid Joseph might accuse them of stealing in addition to being spies.

vv. 29–38
Once his sons return to Canaan, Jacob's sons tell him that the governor spoke harshly toward them and accused them of being spies. They recount what they told Joseph. Jacob's sons tell him that they must return with Benjamin for Simeon to be released from prison. Then they all open their sacks and realize that all of them have had their money restored to them. They become afraid and believe this is punishment for what they have done to Joseph. Jacob becomes depressed because Joseph is gone, Simeon is gone, and now he will have to risk losing Benjamin. Reuben states that he will take personal responsibility for Benjamin and pledges the life of his own two sons. Jacob will not allow Benjamin to go because the sorrow will be too much to bear if something happens to him.

Commentary
This chapter is interesting because we, the readers, are able to see all sides of the story. Joseph's brothers do not recognize him when they arrive in Egypt, and they bow to him and pay him respect. It is at this point that Joseph remembers the dreams that he had as a teenager. His dreams have come true, although it has taken twenty years to occur. At this point, he is thirty-seven years old. When he had the

dreams about the sheaves bowing and the sun, moon, and eleven stars bowing to him, he was seventeen.

I do not think Joseph's actions are to punish his brothers. I believe Joseph has a desire to see Benjamin and to see if his brothers have changed. Joseph's brothers appear to have had a change of attitude and heart since he last saw them. Now they appear to feel guilty for what they did toward Joseph. Even Reuben, once again stepping up as the oldest son, states he will take personal responsibility for his youngest brother if Jacob will allow him to go to Egypt.

Review
1. Why do Joseph's brothers go to Egypt?
2. Does Joseph recognize his brothers immediately?
3. How long does it take for Joseph's original dreams to come true?
4. Who do they have to bring back when they return to Egypt?
5. How does Jacob respond when the brothers return home?

Genesis Chapter 43

1 *And the famine was sore in the land.*
2 And it came to pass, when they had eaten up the corn which they had brought out of Egypt, their father said unto them, Go again, buy us a little food.

3 And Judah spake unto him, saying, The man did solemnly protest unto us, saying, Ye shall not see my face, except your brother be with you.

4 If thou wilt send our brother with us, we will go down and buy thee food:

5 But if thou wilt not send him, we will not go down: for the man said unto us, Ye shall not see my face, except your brother be with you.

6 And Israel said, Wherefore dealt ye so ill with me, as to tell the man whether ye had yet a brother?

7 And they said, The man asked us straitly of our state, and of our kindred, saying, Is your father yet alive? have ye another brother? and we told him according to the tenor of these words: could we certainly know that he would say, Bring your brother down?

8 And Judah said unto Israel his father, Send the lad with me, and we will arise and go; that we may live, and not die, both we, and thou, and also our little ones.

9 I will be surety for him; of my hand shalt thou require him: if I bring him not unto thee, and set him before thee, then let me bear the blame for ever:

10 For except we had lingered, surely now we had returned this second time.

11 And their father Israel said unto them, If it must be so now, do this; take of the best fruits in the land in your vessels, and carry down the man a present, a little balm, and a little honey, spices, and myrrh, nuts, and almonds:

12 And take double money in your hand; and the money that was brought again in the mouth of your sacks, carry it again in your hand; peradventure it was an oversight:

13 Take also your brother, and arise, go again unto the man:

14 And God Almighty give you mercy before the man, that he may send away your other brother, and Benjamin. If I be bereaved of my children, I am bereaved.

15 And the men took that present, and they took double money in their hand, and Benjamin; and rose up, and went down to Egypt, and stood before Joseph.

16 And when Joseph saw Benjamin with them, he said to the ruler of his house, Bring these men home, and slay, and make ready; for these men shall dine with me at noon.

17 And the man did as Joseph bade; and the man brought the men into Joseph's house.

18 And the men were afraid, because they were brought into Joseph's house; and they said, Because of the money that was returned in our sacks at the first time are we brought in; that he may seek occasion against us, and fall upon us, and take us for bondmen, and our asses.

19 And they came near to the steward of Joseph's house, and they communed with him at the door of the house,

20 And said, O sir, we came indeed down at the first time to buy food:

21 And it came to pass, when we came to the inn, that we opened our sacks, and, behold, every man's money was in the mouth of his sack, our money in full weight: and we have brought it again in our hand.

22 And other money have we brought down in our hands to buy food: we cannot tell who put our money in our sacks.

23 And he said, Peace be to you, fear not: your God, and the God of your father, hath given you treasure in your sacks: I had your money. And he brought Simeon out unto them.

24 And the man brought the men into Joseph's house, and gave them water, and they washed their feet; and he gave their asses provender.

25 And they made ready the present against Joseph came at noon: for they heard that they should eat bread there.

26 And when Joseph came home, they brought him the present which was in their hand into the house, and bowed themselves to him to the earth.

27 And he asked them of their welfare, and said, Is your father well, the old man of whom ye spake? Is he yet alive?

28 And they answered, Thy servant our father is in good health, he is yet alive. And they bowed down their heads, and made obeisance.

29 And he lifted up his eyes, and saw his brother Benjamin, his mother's son, and said, Is this your younger brother, of whom ye spake unto me? And he said, God be gracious unto thee, my son.

30 And Joseph made haste; for his bowels did yearn upon his brother: and he sought where to weep; and he entered into his chamber, and wept there.

31 And he washed his face, and went out, and refrained himself, and said, Set on bread.

32 And they set on for him by himself, and for them by themselves, and for the Egyptians, which did eat with him, by themselves: because the Egyptians might not eat bread with the Hebrews; for that is an abomination unto the Egyptians.

33 And they sat before him, the firstborn according to his birthright, and the youngest according to his youth: and the men marvelled one at another.

34 And he took and sent messes unto them from before him: but Benjamin's mess was five times so much as any of theirs. And they drank, and were merry with him.

Summary

vv. 1–14

The famine continues, and Jacob tells his sons to go back to Egypt to buy more food. Judah states that the governor will not receive them unless Benjamin is with them. He states they will not go unless Benjamin comes with them. Israel asks why they told the governor that they have another brother. They reply that the man asked about their father and if they had another brother. They state they just answered honestly and had no idea the man would request that Benjamin come to Egypt. Judah asks Jacob to send Benjamin because otherwise, they will all starve. Judah says he will take personal responsibility if something happens to Benjamin, and they could have been there and back twice by now if they had not wasted time. Finally, Jacob agrees to send them back to Egypt with Benjamin. They leave with twice the money so they can pay for the food from the last visit and the food from this visit. They also bring gifts for the governor. Jacob asks that God will have mercy on them and that Simeon will be released.

vv. 15–30

Joseph's brothers return to Egypt. When Joseph sees Benjamin, he tells his servants to prepare a meal for them at his home to be held at noon. His brothers are brought to Joseph's house. Once his brothers arrive at his house, they are afraid that they will be accused of stealing, their possessions will be seized, and they will become slaves. They talk to Joseph's steward at the door. They say they came there the first time to buy food, but on their way home, they found the money was back in their sacks. They do not know who put the money back. He tells them that their God must have given them back the money, and he brings Simeon out of prison. He brings them into Joseph's house and gives them water to wash their feet and feed their donkeys. They prepare the presents they have for Joseph. When Joseph arrives, they give him the presents and bow before him. He asks about their father, and they tell Joseph their father is doing well. He sees Benjamin and asks if he is their younger brother and says God will be gracious to him.

vv. 31–34

Joseph once again is overwhelmed with emotion and goes into another room and cries. He washes his face and returns. The brothers are seated separately from him because the Egyptians do not eat with Hebrews. His brothers are seated in the order of their birth, and they wonder how Joseph knows this. Although they are all given large portions of food, Benjamin is given five times the amount of the others.

Commentary

As this story continues, we are still privy to all the information while Joseph's brothers do not yet know Joseph's identity. This time, Judah is willing to take personal responsibility for Benjamin's welfare, just as Reuben was willing to do in the previous chapter. Although the text refers to Benjamin as if he is a child, he is approximately seven years younger than Joseph, which makes him about thirty years old.[79]

Now Jacob's sons are a more unified unit in that they are willing to sacrifice for each other. They also exhibit honesty by telling Joseph's steward about the money that was left in their sacks. It appears that they are no longer jealous and vengeful men but men who are honest and compassionate.

Review

1. Who is willing to take personal responsibility for Benjamin's safety at this point?
2. Why are Joseph's brothers afraid when they are brought to his house?
3. What explanation does the steward give the brothers for the money they found in their sacks?
4. Why does Joseph sit separately from his brothers during dinner?
5. Why are Joseph's brother surprised by how they are seated for dinner?

---

[79] Walton, *Genesis*, 667.

Genesis Chapter 44

1 *And he commanded the steward of his house, saying, Fill the men's sacks with food, as much as they can carry, and put every man's money in his sack's mouth.*

2 And put my cup, the silver cup, in the sack's mouth of the youngest, and his corn money. And he did according to the word that Joseph had spoken.

3 As soon as the morning was light, the men were sent away, they and their asses.

4 And when they were gone out of the city, and not yet far off, Joseph said unto his steward, Up, follow after the men; and when thou dost overtake them, say unto them, Wherefore have ye rewarded evil for good?

5 Is not this it in which my lord drinketh, and whereby indeed he divineth? ye have done evil in so doing.

6 And he overtook them, and he spake unto them these same words.

7 And they said unto him, Wherefore saith my lord these words? God forbid that thy servants should do according to this thing:

8 Behold, the money, which we found in our sacks' mouths, we brought again unto thee out of the land of Canaan: how then should we steal out of thy lord's house silver or gold?

9 With whomsoever of thy servants it be found, both let him die, and we also will be my lord's bondmen.

10 And he said, Now also let it be according unto your words: he with whom it is found shall be my servant; and ye shall be blameless.

11 Then they speedily took down every man his sack to the ground, and opened every man his sack.

12 And he searched, and began at the eldest, and left at the youngest: and the cup was found in Benjamin's sack.

13 Then they rent their clothes, and laded every man his ass, and returned to the city.

14 And Judah and his brethren came to Joseph's house; for he was yet there: and they fell before him on the ground.

15 And Joseph said unto them, What deed is this that ye have done? wot ye not that such a man as I can certainly divine?

16 And Judah said, What shall we say unto my lord? what shall we speak? or how shall we clear ourselves? God hath found out the iniquity of thy servants: behold, we are my lord's servants, both we, and he also with whom the cup is found.

17 And he said, God forbid that I should do so: but the man in whose hand the cup is found, he shall be my servant; and as for you, get you up in peace unto your father.

18 Then Judah came near unto him, and said, Oh my lord, let thy servant, I pray thee, speak a word in my lord's ears, and let not thine anger burn against thy servant: for thou art even as Pharaoh.

19 My lord asked his servants, saying, Have ye a father, or a brother?

20 And we said unto my lord, We have a father, an old man, and a child of his old age, a little one; and his brother is dead, and he alone is left of his mother, and his father loveth him.

21 And thou saids unto thy servants, Bring him down unto me, that I may set mine eyes upon him.

22 And we said unto my lord, The lad cannot leave his father: for if he should leave his father, his father would die.

23 And thou saidst unto thy servants, Except your youngest brother come down with you, ye shall see my face no more.

24 And it came to pass when we came up unto thy servant my father, we told him the words of my lord.

25 And our father said, Go again, and buy us a little food.

26 And we said, We cannot go down: if our youngest brother be with us, then will we go down: for we may not see the man's face, except our youngest brother be with us.

27 And thy servant my father said unto us, Ye know that my wife bare me two sons:

28 And the one went out from me, and I said, Surely he is torn in pieces; and I saw him not since:

29 And if ye take this also from me, and mischief befall him, ye shall bring down my gray hairs with sorrow to the grave.

30 Now therefore when I come to thy servant my father, and the lad be not with us; seeing that his life is bound up in the lad's life;

31 It shall come to pass, when he seeth that the lad is not with us, that he will die: and thy servants shall bring down the gray hairs of thy servant our father with sorrow to the grave.

32 For thy servant became surety for the lad unto my father, saying, If I bring him not unto thee, then I shall bear the blame to my father for ever.

33 Now therefore, I pray thee, let thy servant abide instead of the lad a bondman to my lord; and let the lad go up with his brethren.

34 For how shall I go up to my father, and the lad be not with me? lest peradventure I see the evil that shall come on my father.

Summary

vv. 1–2

Joseph tells his steward to put as much food as his brothers can carry and their money back into their sacks and to put his silver cup into Benjamin's sack.

vv. 3–13

The brothers begin to travel back to Canaan. Joseph then orders his servants to catch up with them and ask them if they have repaid evil for good by stealing the master's silver cup. Joseph's brothers say they did not steal the cup. They say they brought back the money they found in their sacks from the first time, so why would they steal? Joseph's servants state that whoever's sack the silver cup is found in will die and that the rest of them will be Joseph's slaves. Joseph replies that only the one who stole the cup will be punished and become a slave. The others will go free. They quickly take down their sacks, and the cup is found in Benjamin's sack. The brothers tear their clothes in mourning and despair and go back to Egypt.

vv. 14–17

Judah and his brothers fall at Joseph's feet. Joseph asks what they have done by allowing this theft. Don't they know Joseph is a man who can predict the future? Judah states they can't explain what happened and that all the brothers except for Benjamin will be his slaves. Joseph says that only the one who stole the cup will be his slave. The others can go back to their father in peace.

vv. 18–34

Judah pleads with Joseph. He states that Joseph asked if they had a father, and they replied that their father is old and has a child from his old age and one who is dead. Benjamin is the only remaining child from his mother, who their father loved. Judah recounts telling Jacob about Joseph's request. Joseph had said that he wanted to see Benjamin. They said Benjamin could not leave their father because their father would die. But Joseph stated that unless they brought Benjamin, they could not see Joseph and buy more food. When they went back home, they told their father what Joseph said. Then Jacob said to go and buy more food. The brothers told Jacob they could not go unless they took Benjamin. Jacob replied that his wife (Rachel) bore him two sons. One went out and was killed by a wild animal, and if something were to happen to Benjamin, he would be grieved unto death. Jacob's life is bound up in Benjamin's life. If they go back home and Jacob sees that Benjamin is not with them, he will die. Judah states he has guaranteed Benjamin's welfare, so he is willing to stay as a slave and let Benjamin and his other brothers return to his father. Judah cannot return home and see how distraught his father will be if Benjamin does not return.

Commentary

At this point, we can see the change in the brothers because now they are willing to sacrifice themselves for the happiness of Jacob. Despite the family dysfunction of favoritism and jealousy, they have grown in that now they are willing to stick together.

Review

1. Why do Joseph's men confront his brothers as they are traveling back to Canaan?
2. Where is the silver cup found?
3. What does Joseph suggest as punishment for the man who has stolen the cup?
4. What is Judah's response once the cup is found?
5. Why does Joseph orchestrate this elaborate plan against his brothers?

Genesis Chapter 45

1 Then Joseph could not refrain himself before all them that stood by him; and he cried, Cause every man to go out from me. And there stood no man with him, while Joseph made himself known unto his brethren.

2 And he wept aloud: and the Egyptians and the house of Pharaoh heard.

3 And Joseph said unto his brethren, I am Joseph; doth my father yet live? And his brethren could not answer him; for they were troubled at his presence.

4 And Joseph said unto his brethren, Come near to me, I pray you. And they came near. And he said I am Joseph your brother, whom ye sold into Egypt.

5 Now therefore be not grieved, nor angry with yourselves, that ye sold me hither: for God did send me before you to preserve life.

6 For these two years hath the famine been in the land: and yet there are five years, in the which there shall neither be earing nor harvest.

7 And God sent me before you to preserve you a posterity in the earth, and to save your lives by a great deliverance.

8 So now it was not you that sent me hither, but God: and he hath made me a father to Pharaoh, and lord of all his house, and a ruler throughout all the land of Egypt.

9 Haste ye, and go up to my father, and say unto him, Thus saith thy son Joseph, God hath made me lord of all Egypt: come down unto me, tarry not:

10 And thou shalt dwell in the land of Goshen, and thou shalt be near unto me, thou, and thy children, and thy children's children, and thy flocks, and thy herds, and all that thou hast:

11 And there will I nourish thee; for yet there are five years of famine; lest thou, and thy household, and all that thou hast, come to poverty.

12 And, behold, your eyes see, and the eyes of my brother Benjamin, that it is my mouth that speaketh unto you.

13 And ye shall tell my father of all my glory in Egypt, and of all that ye have seen; and ye shall haste and bring down my father hither.

14 And he fell upon his brother Benjamin's neck, and wept; and Benjamin wept upon his neck.

15 Moreover he kissed all his brethren, and wept upon them: and after that his brethren talked with him.

16 And the fame thereof was heard in Pharaoh's house, saying, Joseph's brethren are come: and it pleased Pharaoh well, and his servants.

17 And Pharaoh said unto Joseph, Say unto thy brethren, This do ye; lade your beasts, and go, get you unto the land of Canaan;

18 And take your father and your households, and come unto me: and I will give you the good of the land of Egypt, and ye shall eat the fat of the land.

19 Now thou art commanded, this do ye; take you wagons out of the land of Egypt for your little ones, and for your wives, and bring your father, and come.

20 Also regard not your stuff; for the good of all the land of Egypt is yours.

21 And the children of Israel did so: and Joseph gave them wagons, according to the commandment of Pharaoh, and gave them provision for the way.

22 To all of them he gave each man changes of raiment; but to Benjamin he gave three hundred pieces of silver, and five changes of raiment.

23 And to his father he sent after this manner; ten asses laden with the good things of Egypt, and ten she asses laden with corn and bread and meat for his father by the way.

24 So he sent his brethren away, and they departed: and he said unto them, See that ye fall not out by the way.

25 And they went up out of Egypt, and came into the land of Canaan unto Jacob their father,

26 And told him, saying, Joseph is yet alive, and he is governor over all the land of Egypt. And Jacob's heart fainted, for he believed them not.

27 And they told him all the words of Joseph, which he had said unto them: and when he saw the wagons which Joseph had sent to carry him, the spirit of Jacob their father revived:

28 And Israel said, It is enough; Joseph my son is yet alive: I will go and see him before I die.

Summary
vv. 1–8
Joseph can no longer restrain himself and asks for all the servants to leave so that he is alone with his brothers. Joseph becomes overwhelmed with emotion and begins to cry. Joseph finally reveals his identity. He asks about his father. His brothers are stunned and scared about what might happen to them. He assures them that he holds no grudges toward them because he now understands that it was God's will for him to come here to save his family. He tells them that there have been two years of famine and that there will be five more years of famine. Joseph states that God made him ruler in Egypt.

vv. 9–15
Joseph tells his brothers to go back and tell Jacob that God has made him ruler over Egypt. Joseph wants his family to live in Goshen, which is close to Egypt, and he will take care of them all because there are still five more years of famine. Joseph continues by saying that they should know it is him because he is speaking in their own language. Joseph cries and kisses all his brothers, and his brothers talk with him.

vv. 16–25
Pharaoh hears that Joseph's brothers are in Egypt, and he is happy for Joseph. When Pharaoh is told that the rest of Joseph's family is in Canaan, Pharaoh tells Joseph to bring his family to Egypt. Pharaoh will provide wagons, supplies, and lavish gifts for Joseph's family so they can travel to Egypt, and they will be given land. Joseph's brothers return to Canaan.

vv. 26–28
Joseph's brothers tell Jacob that Joseph is alive and that he is governor over Egypt. Jacob is in disbelief. They tell him everything Joseph said, and when Jacob sees the wagons, his spirit is revived. Israel is going to be able to see Joseph before he dies.

Commentary
Joseph's maturity and character are revealed again in this chapter. Although he has every right to be angry toward his brothers, he forgives them and restores their relationship. One of the reasons Joseph forgives his brothers is that he realizes it was God's plan to send him to Egypt to save his family.

Jacob is overcome with emotion about the news that Joseph is alive. From Jacob's perspective, Joseph was dead and now miraculously is alive. Not only is Joseph alive, but he also has come just at the right time to save his family from potential death. Joseph is what is considered to be an Old Testament type of Christ.[80] Old Testament types of Christ are men in the Bible who have some characteristics of Jesus Christ in that they save people or make a sacrifice in a similar though much less significant way to Jesus Christ. These situations are recorded to prepare the way for the true Savior. In Genesis, Noah, Abraham, Isaac, Jacob, and Joseph are types of Christ.

Review
1. What are Joseph's brothers' initial reactions when he reveals his identity?
2. When Pharaoh hears that Joseph's brothers are in Egypt, what is his response?
3. What goods and provisions does Joseph give his brothers for their trip back to Canaan?
4. What presents does Joseph send specifically for his father?
5. What is Jacob's response when he is told Joseph was alive?

---

[80] Daniel J. Cameron, "Typology," in *The Lexham Bible Dictionary*, eds. John D. Barry et al.

Genesis Chapter 46

1   *And Israel took his journey with all that he had, and came to Beer-sheba, and offered sacrifices unto the God of his father Isaac.*

2 And God spake unto Israel in the visions of the night, and said, Jacob, Jacob. And he said, Here am I.

3 And he said, I am God, the God of thy father: fear not to go down into Egypt; for I will there make of thee a great nation:

4 I will go down with thee into Egypt; and I will also surely bring thee up again: and Joseph shall put his hand upon thine eyes.

5 And Jacob rose up from Beer-sheba: and the sons of Israel carried Jacob their father, and their little ones, and their wives, in the wagons which Pharaoh had sent to carry him.

6 And they took their cattle, and their goods, which they had gotten in the land of Canaan, and came into Egypt, Jacob, and all his seed with him:

7 His sons, and his sons' sons with him, his daughters, and his sons' daughters, and all his seed brought he with him into Egypt.

8 And these are the names of the children of Israel, which came into Egypt, Jacob and his sons: Reuben, Jacob's firstborn.

9 And the sons of Reuben; Hanoch, and Phallu, and Hezron, and Carmi.

10 And the sons of Simeon; Jemuel, and Jamin, and Ohad, and Jachin, and Zohar, and Shaul the son of a Canaanitish woman.

11 And the sons of Levi; Gershon, Kohath, and Merari.

12 And the sons of Judah; Er, and Onan, and Shelah, and Pharez, and Zarah: but Er and Onan died in the land of Canaan. And the sons of Pharez were Hezron and Hamul.

13 And the sons of Issachar; Tola, and Phuvah, and Job, and Shimron.

14 And the sons of Zebulun; Sered, and Elon, and Jahleel.

15 These be the sons of Leah, which she bare unto Jacob in Padan-aram, with his daughter Dinah: all the souls of his sons and his daughters were thirty and three.

16 And the sons of Gad; Ziphion, and Haggi, Shuni, and Ezbon, Eri, and Arodi, and Areli.

17 And the sons of Asher; Jimnah, and Ishuah, and Isui, and Beriah, and Serah their sister: and the sons of Beriah; Heber, and Malchiel.

18 These are the sons of Zilpah, whom Laban gave to Leah his daughter, and these she bare unto Jacob, even sixteen souls.

19 The sons of Rachel Jacob's wife; Joseph, and Benjamin.

20 And unto Joseph in the land of Egypt were born Manasseh and Ephraim, which Asenath the daughter of Poti-pherah priest of On bare unto him.

21 And the sons of Benjamin were Belah, and Becher, and Ashbel, Gera, and Naaman, Ehi, and Rosh, Muppim, and Huppim, and Ard.

22 These are the sons of Rachel, which were born to Jacob: all the souls were fourteen.

23 And the sons of Dan; Hushim.

24 And the sons of Naphtali; Jahzeel, and Guni, and Jezer, and Shillem.

25 These are the sons of Bilhah, which Laban gave unto Rachel his daughter, and she bare unto Jacob: all the souls were seven.

26 All the souls that came with Jacob into Egypt, which came out of his loins, besides Jacob's sons' wives, all the souls were threescore and six;

27 And the sons of Joseph, which were born him in Egypt, were two souls: all the souls of the house of Jacob, which came into Egypt, were threescore and ten.

28 And he sent Judah before him unto Joseph, to direct his face unto Goshen; and they came into the land of Goshen.

29 And Joseph made ready his chariot, and went up to meet Israel his father, to Goshen, and presented himself unto him; and he fell on his neck, and wept on his neck a good while.

30 And Israel said unto Joseph, Now let me die, since I have seen thy face, because thou art yet alive.

31 And Joseph said unto his brethren, and unto his father's house, I will go up, and shew Pharaoh, and say unto him, My brethren, and my father's house, which were in the land of Canaan, are come unto me;

32 And the men are shepherds, for their trade hath been to feed cattle; and they have brought their flocks, and their herds, and all that they have.

33 And it shall come to pass, when Pharaoh shall call you, and shall say, What is your occupation?

34 That ye shall say, Thy servants' trade hath been about cattle from our youth even until now, both we, and also our fathers: that ye may dwell in the land of Goshen; for every shepherd is an abomination unto the Egyptians.

Summary
vv. 1–4
Israel starts to travel toward Egypt and comes to Beersheba and offers sacrifices to God. God speaks to him and says not to be afraid to go to Egypt because God is going to make them a great nation. God also states that Israel will be able to see Joseph before he dies.

vv. 5–7
Jacob leaves Beersheba, and his sons take him and their family in the wagons that Pharaoh has sent, and they travel to Egypt. They take all their cattle and all their possessions.

vv. 8–15
These verses list the names of Leah's children and their children. The total is thirty-three.

vv. 16–18
These are the names of the sons and their children born from Zilpah, Leah's maidservant. Their total is sixteen.

vv. 19–22
These are the names of the sons and their children born from Rachel. Their total is fourteen.

vv. 23–25
This is the list of the sons and their children born from Bilhah, Rachel's handmaid. Their total is seven.

vv. 26–27
All of Jacob's family is counted, and the total is sixty-six. When Joseph and his sons, plus Jacob, are included, Jacob's family totals seventy people.

vv. 28–34

Jacob sends Judah ahead of them to meet Joseph and get directions to the land of Goshen. Joseph and Israel are finally reunited, and it is very emotional. They both cry and hold each other for a long time. Israel says now he can die since he has seen Joseph and knows he is alive. Joseph tells his family that he is going to go and tell Pharaoh that his family has come to be close to him. Joseph will state that they are shepherds and that they have brought their herds and cattle. When Pharaoh asks them what their occupation is, they should tell him that they have been shepherds since they were young just as their ancestors were so they will be able to live in Goshen. Shepherds were looked down upon by the Egyptians.

Commentary

As Israel prepares to go to Egypt, God speaks to him. God identifies Himself as the God of Isaac. God tells Israel not to be afraid and to go to Egypt because He is going to make Israel's family a great nation.[81] This incident is in contrast to when Isaac was going to go to Egypt because there was a famine in Canaan. God told Isaac not to go to Egypt in Genesis 26 but to stay in the land of Canaan, and He would bless him. Here, God is telling Israel He is going to bless them in Egypt. We can see the continuation of the covenant blessing that God gave to Abraham being passed on to Jacob.

After this blessing, the descendants of Israel are counted. Although the descendants of Abraham through Isaac and now through Jacob are not yet as the stars in the sky or the sand of the seashore, they now total seventy. This total grows to 600,000 men[82] with an estimated two million people total, including women and children, when they finally leave Egypt.[83] Although none of the patriarchs live to see this generational blessing manifest, they do see God's supernatural intervention in the lives of each patriarch.

Review
1. Why might Jacob be afraid to go to Egypt?
2. What does God say to Jacob about going to Egypt?
3. What is the number of Jacob's family who go to Egypt?
4. Describe what happens when Jacob and Joseph finally see each other.

---

[81] This is a generational blessing—a blessing that is passed on from generation to generation until it is fulfilled.

[82] Exodus 12:37

[83] Walter C. Kaiser Jr., "Exodus," in *The Expositor's Bible Commentary*, vol. 2, *Genesis, Exodus, Leviticus, Numbers*, ed. Frank E. Gaebelein (Grand Rapids: Zondervan, 1990), 379.

5. What does Joseph instruct his brothers to say when Pharaoh asks about their occupation?

Genesis Chapter 47

1 *Then Joseph came and told Pharaoh, and said, My father and my brethren, and their flocks, and their herds, and all that they have, are come out of the land of Canaan; and, behold, they are in the land of Goshen.*

2 And he took some of his brethren, even five men, and presented them unto Pharaoh.

3 And Pharaoh said unto his brethren, What is your occupation? And they said unto Pharaoh, Thy servants are shepherds, both we, and also our fathers.

4 They said moreover unto Pharaoh, For to sojourn in the land are we come; for thy servants have no pasture for their flocks; for the famine is sore in the land of Canaan: now therefore, we pray thee, let thy servants dwell in the land of Goshen.

5 And Pharaoh spake unto Joseph, saying, Thy father and thy brethren are come unto thee:

6 The land of Egypt is before thee; in the best of the land make thy father and brethren to dwell; in the land of Goshen let them dwell: and if thou knowest any men of activity among them, then make them rulers over my cattle.

7 And Joseph brought in Jacob his father, and set him before Pharaoh: and Jacob blessed Pharaoh.

8 And Pharaoh said unto Jacob, How old art thou?

9 And Jacob said unto Pharaoh, The days of the years of my pilgrimage are an hundred and thirty years: few and evil have the days of the years of my life been, and have not attained unto the days of the years of the life of my fathers in the days of their pilgrimage.

10 And Jacob blessed Pharaoh, and went out from before Pharaoh.

11 And Joseph placed his father and his brethren, and gave them a possession in the land of Egypt, in the best of the land, in the land of Rameses, as Pharaoh had commanded.

12 And Joseph nourished his father, and his brethren, and all his father's household, with bread, according to their families.

13 And there was no bread in all the land; for the famine was very sore, so that the land of Egypt and all the land of Canaan fainted by reason of the famine.

14 And Joseph gathered up all the money that was found in the land of Egypt, and in the land of Canaan, for the corn which they bought: and Joseph brought the money into Pharaoh's house.

15 And when money failed in the land of Egypt, and in the land of Canaan, all the Egyptians came unto Joseph, and said, Give us bread: for why should we die in thy presence? for the money faileth.

16 And Joseph said, Give your cattle; and I will give you for your cattle, if money fail.

17 And they brought their cattle unto Joseph: and Joseph gave them bread in exchange for horses, and for the flocks, and for the cattle of the herds, and for the asses: and he fed them with bread for all their cattle for that year.

18 When that year was ended, they came unto him the second year, and said unto him, We will not hide it from my lord, how that our money is spent; my lord also hath our herds of cattle; there is not ought left in the sight of my lord, but our bodies, and our lands:

19 Wherefore shall we die before thine eyes, both we and our land? buy us and our land for bread, and we and our land will be servants unto Pharaoh: and give us seed, that we may live, and not die, that the land be not desolate.

20 And Joseph bought all the land of Egypt for Pharaoh; for the Egyptians sold every man his field, because the famine prevailed over them: so the land became Pharaoh's.

21 And as for the people, he removed them to cities from one end of the borders of Egypt even to the other end thereof.

22 Only the land of the priests bought he not; for the priests had a portion assigned them of Pharaoh, and did eat their portion which Pharaoh gave them: wherefore they sold not their lands.

23 Then Joseph said unto the people, Behold, I have bought you this day and your land for Pharaoh: lo, here is seed for you, and ye shall sow the land.

24 And it shall come to pass in the increase, that ye shall give the fifth part unto Pharaoh, and four parts shall be your own, for seed of the field, and for your food, and for them of your households, and for food for your little ones.

25 And they said, Thou hast saved our lives: let us find grace in the sight of my lord, and we will be Pharaoh's servants.

26 And Joseph made it a law over the land of Egypt unto this day, that Pharaoh should have the fifth part; except the land of the priests only, which became not Pharaoh's.

27 And Israel dwelt in the land of Egypt, in the country of Goshen; and they had possessions therein, and grew, and multiplied exceedingly.

28 And Jacob lived in the land of Egypt seventeen years: so the whole age of Jacob was an hundred forty and seven years.

29 And the time drew nigh that Israel must die: and he called his son Joseph, and said unto him, If now I have found grace in thy sight, put, I pray thee, thy hand under my thigh, and deal kindly and truly with me; bury me not, I pray thee, in Egypt:

30 But I will lie with my fathers, and thou shalt carry me out of Egypt, and bury me in their burying place. And he said, I will do as thou hast said.

31 And he said, Swear unto me. And he sware unto him. And Israel bowed himself upon the bed's head.

Summary

vv. 1–6

Joseph tells Pharaoh that his father and brothers and their flocks came from Canaan and are now in Goshen. Joseph presents five of his brothers to Pharaoh. Pharaoh asks their occupation, and they respond that they are shepherds. They have come because the famine is great in Canaan, and they would like to live in Goshen. Pharaoh tells Joseph that they may live in Goshen and they can even be in charge of Pharaoh's cattle.

vv. 7–12

Joseph presents his father to Pharaoh. Pharaoh asks Jacob's age. Jacob states he is 130 years old. Jacob says his life has been difficult and shorter than his ancestors' lives. Jacob blesses Pharaoh. Joseph has his family settle in Goshen, and he provides for them.

vv. 13–26

Eventually, there is no food in Canaan or in Egypt because the famine is very severe. Joseph gathers all the money that has been acquired from selling the corn and brings it to Pharaoh. Since the Egyptians' money has dwindled and they cannot afford to buy food, Joseph accepts cattle in exchange for food. The Egyptians have enough cattle to provide food for themselves for another year. When the Egyptians have no more cattle, Joseph accepts land in exchange for food. The Egyptians will give the profit of one fifth of the land they farm to Pharaoh in exchange for food. The only exception is the Egyptian priests. Their land cannot be sold because Pharaoh has given it to them.

vv. 27–31

Israel's family prospers in the land of Goshen. Jacob lives there for seventeen years, so at the time of his death, he is 147 years old. Jacob is getting older and will soon die. He asks Joseph to promise that he will bury Jacob with his ancestors, and Joseph states that he will.

Commentary

Now Israel and his family are settled in Goshen and become prosperous, just as God has said to Israel. As Israel gets older, he has Joseph promise to bury him with his ancestors in the land of Canaan, which is the land that God has promised Israel and his descendants. This is a foreshadowing that his descendants will not be living in Egypt permanently and will one day live in the land God has promised them. Once again, we see the pledge of an oath by placing the hand underneath the thigh.

We can see that Pharaoh's decision to put Joseph in charge during the famine was a wise one. Joseph is able to increase Pharaoh's wealth and also feed the people.

Review

1. What land does Pharaoh give to Joseph's family? Why that particular area?
2. What does Jacob mean in Genesis 47:9 when he states, "few and evil have the days of my life been"?
3. When there is no more bread in the land, what does Joseph do next?
4. Why doesn't Joseph buy the priests' land for Pharaoh?
5. What promise does Joseph make to Jacob concerning his death and burial?

Genesis Chapter 48

1 *And it came to pass after these things, that one told Joseph, Behold, thy father is sick: and he took with him his two sons, Manasseh and Ephraim.*
2 And one told Jacob, and said, Behold, thy son Joseph cometh unto thee:
and Israel strengthened himself, and sat upon the bed.

3 And Jacob said unto Joseph, God Almighty appeared unto me at Luz in the land of Canaan, and blessed me,

4 And said unto me, Behold, I will make thee fruitful, and multiply thee, and I will make of thee a multitude of people; and will give this land to thy seed after thee for an everlasting possession.

5 And now thy two sons, Ephraim and Manasseh, which were born unto thee in the land of Egypt before I came unto thee into Egypt, are mine; as Reuben and Simeon, they shall be mine.

6 And thy issue, which thou begettest after them, shall be thine, and shall be called after the name of their brethren in their inheritance.

7 And as for me, when I came from Padan, Rachel died by me in the land of Canaan in the way, when yet there was but a little way to come unto Ephrath: and I buried her there in the way of Ephrath; the same is Beth-lehem.

8 And Israel beheld Joseph's sons, and said, Who are these?

9 And Joseph said unto his father, They are my sons, whom God hath given me in this place. And he said, Bring them, I pray thee, unto me, and I will bless them.

10 Now the eyes of Israel were dim for age, so that he could not see. And he brought them near unto him; and he kissed them, and embraced them.

11 And Israel said unto Joseph, I had not thought to see thy face: and, lo, God hath shewed me also thy seed.

12 And Joseph brought them out from between his knees, and he bowed himself with his face to the earth.

13 And Joseph took them both, Ephraim in his right hand toward Israel's left hand, and Manasseh in his left hand toward Israel's right hand, and brought them near unto him.

14 And Israel stretched out his right hand, and laid it upon Ephraim's head, who was the younger, and his left hand upon Manasseh's head, guiding his hands wittingly; for Manasseh was the firstborn.

15 And he blessed Joseph, and said, God, before whom my fathers Abraham and Isaac did walk, the God which fed me all my life long unto this day,

16 The Angel which redeemed me from all evil, bless the lads; and let my name be named on them, and the name of my fathers Abraham and Isaac; and let them grow into a multitude in the midst of the earth.

17 And when Joseph saw that his father laid his right hand upon the head of Ephraim, it displeased him: and he held up his father's hand, to remove it from Ephraim's head unto Manasseh's head.

18 And Joseph said unto his father, Not so, my father: for this is the firstborn; put thy right hand upon his head.

19 And his father refused, and said, I know it, my son, I know it: he also shall become a people, and he also shall be great: but truly his younger brother shall be greater than he, and his seed shall become a multitude of nations.

20 And he blessed them that day, saying, In thee shall Israel bless, saying, God make thee as Ephraim and as Manasseh: and he set Ephraim before Manasseh.

21 And Israel said unto Joseph, Behold, I die: but God shall be with you, and bring you again unto the land of your fathers.

22 Moreover I have given to thee one portion above thy brethren, which I took out of the hand of the Amorite with my sword and with my bow.

Summary

vv. 1–2

Joseph is informed that Jacob is sick, and Joseph takes his two sons, Manasseh and Ephraim, to visit Jacob. Jacob is told that Joseph has come to visit him. He strengthens himself and sits up in the bed.

vv. 3–7

Jacob begins by recalling how God appeared to him in Luz (Bethel) and blessed him and said he would be fruitful and multiply him and give Canaan to his descendants (generational blessing). Jacob continues by stating that Joseph's sons, Manasseh and Ephraim, who were born to Joseph in Egypt, would be his sons like Reuben and Simeon. Any sons Joseph has after these two will be Joseph's sons to carry on his family line. Jacob states that Rachel died on the way to Ephrath and that he buried her in Bethlehem.

vv. 8–22

Israel sees Joseph's sons and asks who they are. Joseph states that they are the sons God gave him in Egypt. Israel says he will bless them. Israel is old and cannot see well, so Joseph brings his sons close so Israel can hug and kiss them. Israel states he is grateful because he did not think he would ever see Joseph again. Not only has he been able to see Joseph, but he's also seen Joseph's sons. Joseph bows before Israel and takes Ephraim to a place on Israel's left hand and Manasseh to Israel's right hand. However, Israel puts his right hand on Ephraim, who is the youngest, and his left hand on Manasseh, who is the oldest. Israel blesses Joseph and blesses Joseph's son. He states that the God of Abraham and Isaac and the God who has been with him will multiply them. Joseph recognizes that Israel has his right hand on Ephraim and the left on Manasseh and tries to switch his hands. But Jacob refuses and says the younger son will be greater than the older. Jacob states that he will die soon but God will bring Joseph back to Canaan. Jacob gives Joseph a double portion of his blessing, including a double portion of the land that Jacob has acquired in Canaan.

Commentary

In this chapter, Israel is giving Joseph the birthright of the oldest son. Joseph is given a double portion of the blessing, which includes land. Israel essentially adopts Ephraim and Manasseh as his own sons. When the Israelites leave Egypt and settle in the Promised Land, the people are identified by their tribes, which are named after the sons of Jacob. There is no tribe named *Joseph* because Jacob adopts Joseph's sons as his own. The half tribes of Ephraim and Manasseh make up the tribe of Joseph.

This chapter is very similar to chapter 27 when Isaac blesses Jacob. Just like Isaac, Jacob is old and does not have good vision, so the sons have to come close to him. Also, just like the blessings of Jacob and Esau, the younger one is going to be greater than the older one. Obviously, this birthright blessing is different in that there is no deception. Israel takes Ephraim and Manasseh as his sons and blesses them just like he had been blessed by his father Isaac.

We see a pattern throughout Genesis that although the birthright should go to the oldest son, that is not a set rule. Whether it is because of sin, such as in the case of Cain and Reuben, or God's choice, as in the case of Isaac and Jacob, many times God chooses the younger or the "least" to be the greatest or most prominent.

Review
1. Why does Jacob call Joseph to come and see him?
2. Discuss Genesis 48:4 with regard to Genesis 12:12, 17:6, and Genesis 26:4.
3. Why is there no tribe of Israel called Joseph?
4. What are the similarities in the roles and outcomes of Esau and Jacob compared to Manasseh and Ephraim?
5. Why does Jacob give Joseph a double portion compared to his brothers?

Genesis Chapter 49

1   *And Jacob called unto his sons, and said, Gather yourselves together, that I may tell you that which shall befall you in the last days.*

2 Gather yourselves together, and hear, ye sons of Jacob; and hearken unto Israel your father.

3 Reuben, thou art my firstborn, my might, and the beginning of my strength, the excellency of dignity, and the excellency of power:

4 Unstable as water, thou shalt not excel; because thou wentest up to thy father's bed; then defiledst thou it: he went up to my couch.

5 Simeon and Levi are brethren; instruments of cruelty are in their habitations.

6 O my soul, come not thou into their secret; unto their assembly, mine honour, be not thou united: for in their anger they slew a man, and in their selfwill they digged down a wall.

7 Cursed be their anger, for it was fierce; and their wrath, for it was cruel: I will divide them in Jacob, and scatter them in Israel.

8 Judah, thou art he whom thy brethren shall praise: thy hand shall be in the neck of thine enemies; thy father's children shall bow down before thee.

9 Judah is a lion's whelp: from the prey, my son, thou art gone up: he stooped down, he couched as a lion, and as an old lion; who shall rouse him up?

10 The sceptre shall not depart from Judah, nor a lawgiver from between his feet, until Shiloh come; and unto him shall the gathering of the people be.

11 Binding his foal unto the vine, and his ass's colt unto the choice vine; he washed his garments in wine, and his clothes in the blood of grapes:

12 His eyes shall be red with wine, and his teeth white with milk.

13 Zebulun shall dwell at the haven of the sea; and he shall be for an haven of ships; and his border shall be unto Zidon.

14 Issachar is a strong ass couching down between two burdens:

15 And he saw that rest was good, and the land that it was pleasant; and bowed his shoulder to bear, and became a servant unto tribute.

16 Dan shall judge his people, as one of the tribes of Israel.

17 Dan shall be a serpent by the way, an adder in the path, that biteth the horse heels, so that his rider shall fall backward.

18 I have waited for thy salvation, O LORD.

19 Gad, a troop shall overcome him: but he shall overcome at the last.

20 Out of Asher his bread shall be fat, and he shall yield royal dainties.

21 Naphtali is a hind let loose: he giveth goodly words.

22 Joseph is a fruitful bough, even a fruitful bough by a well; whose branches run over the wall:

23 The archers have sorely grieved him, and shot at him, and hated him:

24 But his bow abode in strength, and the arms of his hands were made strong by the hands of the mighty God of Jacob; (from thence is the shepherd, the stone of Israel:)

25 Even by the God of thy father, who shall help thee; and by the Almighty, who shall bless thee with blessings of heaven above, blessings of the deep that lieth under, blessings of the breasts, and of the womb:

26 The blessings of thy father have prevailed above the blessings of my progenitors unto the utmost bound of the everlasting hills: they shall be on the head of Joseph, and on the crown of the head of him that was separate from his brethren.

27 Benjamin shall ravin as a wolf: in the morning he shall devour the prey, and at night he shall divide the spoil.

28 All these are the twelve tribes of Israel: and this is it that their father spake unto them, and blessed them; every one according to his blessing he blessed them.

29 And he charged them, and said unto them, I am to be gathered unto my people: bury me with my fathers in the cave that is in the field of Ephron the Hittite,

30 In the cave that is in the field of Machpelah, which is before Mamre, in the land of Canaan, which Abraham bought with the field of Ephron the Hittite for a possession of a buryingplace.

31 There they buried Abraham and Sarah his wife; there they buried Isaac and Rebekah his wife; and there I buried Leah.

32 The purchase of the field and of the cave that is therein was from the children of Heth.

33 And when Jacob had made an end of commanding his sons, he gathered up his feet into the bed, and yielded up the ghost, and was gathered unto his people.

Summary

vv. 1–2

Jacob gathers all his sons together to give each his blessing.

vv. 3–4

Reuben is the firstborn. Reuben represents Jacob's strength, might, and dignity. But Reuben is unstable, so he will not excel. Reuben will not have the rights of the firstborn because he had sexual relations with Bilhah, who was Rachel's handmaid (Gen 35:22).

vv. 5–7

Simeon and Levi are violent. Simeon and Levi are cursed because of their anger. They are the brothers who killed the men after Dinah was sexually assaulted (Gen 34). They will be divided and scattered among Israel.

vv. 8–12

Judah is blessed and praised. This tribe will dominate their enemies, and the other tribes will submit to them. Leadership will come from this tribe, including the Messiah, Jesus Christ.

v. 13

Zebulun's borders will extend to Zidon.

vv. 14–15

Issachar will have a land that is pleasant but will end up submitting to forced labor.

vv. 16–18

Dan will judge his people.

v. 19

Gad's descendants will be attacked and will attack and have victory over their enemies.

v. 20

Asher will enjoy abundance.

v. 21

Naphtali will say beautiful words.

vv. 22–26

Although many things may come against Joseph, he is still abundantly blessed.

v. 27

The tribe of Benjamin will be aggressive and have victory over his enemies.

vv. 28–33

These are the twelve tribes of Israel. Jacob tells them he wants to be buried in the cave of Ephron the Hittite. There they buried Abraham, Sarah, Isaac, Rebekah, and Leah. Abraham purchased the field and cave from the children of Heth. Jacob dies surrounded by his family.

Commentary

Jacob gathers all his sons to bestow blessings on them. The blessings bestowed are in relation to the tribe that each son will become. Because of their behavior, Reuben, Simeon, and Levi are not eligible for the honor of the birthright of the oldest son. The fourth son, Judah, essentially becomes the lead tribe of Israel. This explains why Jesus comes from the tribe of Judah and why the tribe of Reuben is not considered the lead tribe. [84] The tribe of Simeon becomes scattered within the land of Judah [85] Levites also have cities scattered throughout Israel because they are the tribe that serves as priests.

Judah is described as a lion. Jacob also states that thy brethren shall praise him, which is also a characteristic of Judah's future descendant Jesus. Although Joseph is the son who saved his family in this generation, it will be through Judah that the descendants of Israel will be blessed by the Messiah, Jesus Christ.

Some of the descriptions of blessings may seem unusual to the modern reader, but to the Israelites, the terminology was well understood. Zebulun's territory never borders the sea, so it does not seem that this blessing is related to water. Some scholars believe it refers to Zebulun being a leader in trade involving

---

[84] 1 Chronicles 5:1-2
[85] Joshua 19:1-9

seagoing activities.[86] Issachar will settle in good territory but will become enslaved. The tribe of Issachar does settle in fertile land.[87] In the blessing of Dan, there is a play on words with Dan's name, which means "to judge." Dan is compared to a serpent that is small but powerful, an idea that may be applied to the future tribe of Dan. The future tribe of Gad will be involved in war, and they eventually will become famous for military victories.[88] Asher will enjoy affluence. Naphtali also will be blessed. Joseph has been attacked from within his own family and by those in Egypt. Despite opposition in Joseph's life, he is still blessed and considered "a prince" among his brothers in that he assumes the leadership role. Benjamin is described as a "ravenous wolf," which alludes to the future tribe of Benjamin's military greatness.[89]

Although the exact meanings of all the blessings that Jacob declared to his sons are not universally clear, the significance is that Jacob is stating how each tribe will be blessed in their own way. These blessings were significant to the Israelites as they identified themselves by their tribe. The modern reader also gains a greater understanding of the relationships between the tribes and the historical significance of the tribes of Israel.

Review

1. Why does Jacob gather all his sons together?
2. Why does Reuben not obtain the blessing of the firstborn?
3. What do Simeon and Levi do that interferes with them obtaining the blessing of the firstborn?
4. Why does the tribe of Judah become the lead tribe? And who is the most significant person born from this tribe?
5. Why was the blessing given to each tribe significant to the Israelites at that time and to us today?

---

[86] Wenham, *Word Biblical Commentary*, 1:489.

[87] Joshua 19:17-24

[88] 1 Chronicles 5:18, 12:8

[89] Wenham, *Word Biblical Commentary*, 1:487.

Genesis Chapter 50

1 *And Joseph fell upon his father's face, and wept upon him, and kissed him. 2 And Joseph commanded his servants the physicians to embalm his father: and the physicians embalmed Israel.*

3 And forty days were fulfilled for him; for so are fulfilled the days of those which are embalmed: and the Egyptians mourned for him threescore and ten days.

4 And when the days of his mourning were past, Joseph spake unto the house of Pharaoh, saying, If now I have found grace in your eyes, speak, I pray you, in the ears of Pharaoh, saying,

5 My father made me swear, saying, Lo, I die: in my grave which I have digged for me in the land of Canaan, there shalt thou bury me. Now therefore let me go up, I pray thee, and bury my father, and I will come again.

6 And Pharaoh said, Go up, and bury thy father, according as he made thee swear.

7 And Joseph went up to bury his father: and with him went up all the servants of Pharaoh, the elders of his house, and all the elders of the land of Egypt,

8 And all the house of Joseph, and his brethren, and his father's house: only their little ones, and their flocks, and their herds, they left in the land of Goshen.

9 And there went up with him both chariots and horsemen: and it was a very great company.

10 And they came to the threshingfloor of Atad, which is beyond Jordan, and there they mourned with a great and very sore lamentation: and he made a mourning for his father seven days.

11 And when the inhabitants of the land, the Canaanites, saw the mourning in the floor of Atad, they said, This is a grievous mourning to the Egyptians: wherefore the name of it was called Abel-mizraim, which is beyond Jordan.

12 And his sons did unto him according as he commanded them:

13 For his sons carried him into the land of Canaan, and buried him in the cave of the field of Machpelah, which Abraham bought with the field for a possession of a buryingplace of Ephron the Hittite, before Mamre.

14 And Joseph returned into Egypt, he, and his brethren, and all that went up with him to bury his father, after he had buried his father.

15 And when Joseph's brethren saw that their father was dead, they said, Joseph will peradventure hate us, and will certainly requite us all the evil which we did unto him.

16 And they sent a messenger unto Joseph, saying, Thy father did command before he died, saying,

17 So shall ye say unto Joseph, Forgive, I pray thee now, the trespass of thy brethren, and their sin; for they did unto thee evil: and now, we pray thee, forgive the trespass of the servants of the God of thy father. And Joseph wept when they spake unto him.

18 And his brethren also went and fell down before his face; and they said, Behold, we be thy servants.

19 And Joseph said unto them, Fear not: for am I in the place of God?

20 But as for you, ye thought evil against me; but God meant it unto good, to bring to pass, as it is this day, to save much people alive.

21 Now therefore fear ye not: I will nourish you, and your little ones. And he comforted them, and spake kindly unto them.

22 And Joseph dwelt in Egypt, he, and his father's house: and Joseph lived an hundred and ten years.

23 And Joseph saw Ephraim's children of the third generation: the children also of Machir the son of Manasseh were brought up upon Joseph's knees.

24 And Joseph said unto his brethren, I die: and God will surely visit you, and bring you out of this land unto the land which he sware to Abraham, to Isaac, and to Jacob.

25 And Joseph took an oath of the children of Israel, saying, God will surely visit you, and ye shall carry up my bones from hence.

26 So Joseph died, being an hundred and ten years old: and they embalmed him, and he was put in a coffin in Egypt.

Summary

vv. 1–13

Joseph kisses his father and cries. Joseph orders that his father's body be embalmed. The Israelites and the Egyptians mourn for Jacob for forty days. Joseph asks Pharaoh for permission to bury his father in the land of Canaan. Pharaoh gives his permission. Joseph, his servants, and his family and cattle travel to Canaan, and they mourn there for seven more days. When the Canaanites see how intense their grief is for Jacob, they name the area Abel-mizraim. Jacob's sons do as he asked and bury him in Canaan. Jacob is buried in the same cave that Abraham bought from Ephron the Hittite.

vv. 14–21

Joseph and his brothers return to Egypt after they bury their father. Joseph's brothers are afraid now that Jacob is dead that Joseph will treat them badly. Joseph's brothers send a message to him stating that their father said he should forgive them. Joseph cries when they say this to him. Joseph tells them he has forgiven them. He states that he is not God. He also realizes that, although what his brothers did was wrong, it was a part of God's plan to keep their family alive. He reassures them that he will take care of them and their children and speaks nicely to them.

vv. 22–26

Joseph spends the rest of his life in Egypt and dies at 110 years old. Joseph sees the third generation of Ephraim's children and Manasseh's children. Before he dies, Joseph tells his brothers God will take care of them and bring them back to the land that God promised Abraham, Isaac, and Jacob. Joseph makes them promise that when God brings them back to Canaan they will take his bones with them and bury him in Canaan. Joseph dies at 110 years old and is embalmed and placed in a coffin in Egypt.

Commentary

Because of Joseph, Jacob is given the respect of a dignitary in Egypt. Jacob is buried in the same cave as Abraham, Sarah, Isaac, Rebekah, and Leah. His desire to be buried in this cave signifies that this is the land that God has promised his descendants and that they will return to claim their inheritance.

Now that Jacob is dead, Joseph's brothers are concerned that Joseph will finally take revenge for how they treated him in the past. Although selling a brother into slavery is extreme, we can see that the favoritism and sibling rivalry in this family have been going on for generations. Some might even say that it was Jacob's favoritism of Joseph that incited his brothers' hatred of him and precipitated them selling him to the Ishmaelites. But regardless, Joseph acts honorably and with integrity and states that he is not in the place of God, implying that it is not his job to punish his brothers. If there is going to be punishment, then it is God who will judge them. As modern Christians, this is also the attitude we should adopt. The Bible commands us to forgive. Many times we feel that if we forgive someone, they do not have to suffer from the consequences of their actions, but that is not the case. We are commanded to forgive because we are to show love as God loves, and just as He forgives us, we should forgive others. God is the perfect judge and will punish them accordingly. After all, if we were punished for our sins, our punishment would be death.[90]

Verse 20 is a very popular verse that summarizes the purpose of Joseph's life. Although his brothers wanted Joseph to suffer, it was all part of God's plan for the good of Joseph and his family. Joseph is one example where we can describe his character as nearly perfect. We do not see him lie, he does not give in to sexual temptation, and he forgives and cares for his brothers even after they have sold him into slavery. The only thing we might say about Joseph is that he may have been naive and arrogant when he was young and told his family about his dreams. But he does not exhibit any negative actions that are recorded.

Genesis ends with the death of Joseph and the promise of his brothers to bring his bones out of Egypt to be buried in Canaan. This implies that Abraham's descendants will return to Canaan and possess the land. This promise was fulfilled by Moses and Joshua. Joseph's bones are taken out of Egypt, and he is buried in Shechem.[91]

Review
1. Describe how the death of Jacob is treated by the Egyptians.
2. Where is Jacob buried?
3. What do Joseph's brothers fear once Jacob has died?
4. What is Joseph's response to his brothers (Genesis 50:19-20)?
5. How old is Joseph when he dies?

---

[90] Romans 6:23
[91] Exodus 13:19, Joshua 24:32

Conclusion

Genesis begins by describing how God interacts with the totality of humanity but ends by focusing on one family. Genesis describes the creation of the universe and the earth, but—most importantly—Genesis describes the creation of man. Genesis gives us the purpose of mankind and his relationship with God. Genesis answers the questions of why man was created, who created man, and what the purpose of life is. Man was created by God to have fellowship with Him. Although Genesis begins with creation, Genesis ends by emphasizing redemption and salvation.

There are many significant characters in Genesis, but there is a transition starting in chapter 12 when God focuses on Abraham and his descendants. Although God fulfills the promise to Abraham that he and Sarah would have a son, the total manifestation of the other promises are not fulfilled until much later. The promise that God makes to Abraham is that of many descendants, that his name will be great, and that the land of Canaan will be his descendants' possession. When God later appears to Moses and identifies Himself as the God of Abraham, Isaac, and Jacob, we understand that to the Israelites, Abraham's name was great. And now as Christians, we acknowledge Abraham as a great man of faith. When the Israelites left Egypt, they were estimated to be 600,000 men[92] with an estimated two million people total, including women and children.[93] This

---

[92] Exodus 12:37
[93] Kaiser, "Exodus," *The Expositor's Bible Commentary*, 379.

event occurs approximately five hundred years after God first gave this promise to Abraham. Approximately forty years later, the Israelites possessed the land God promised Abraham.

Genesis covers a long period of time in relatively few chapters. It starts with literally "nothing" and ends with a chosen family that will grow into a chosen nation. Although there is a large amount of information in Genesis, I believe it is crucial in understanding who God is and why we need salvation. In my opinion, many people (including Christians) find much of the Old Testament boring and difficult to understand. What I have realized is that when one understands the book of Genesis, the rest of the Bible is much easier to comprehend. Not only is Genesis the beginning, but it is also the foundation to understanding God, the Bible, and the Christian faith.

Now that we understand the events of Genesis, we understand their significance. Genesis establishes that God is both creator and redeemer of mankind. Genesis establishes the foundation of Christianity which is faith and obedience to God. Genesis establishes the plan of redemption and salvation. God chooses one man and it is through his descendants that Jesus Christ is born. It is by Jesus Christ's sacrificial death for the sins of mankind that we have the opportunity of salvation. Genesis establishes that despite mankind's choice to sin that God's love for us was always to restore us to the perfect relationship we had with him *In the Beginning*.

Review
1. How does Genesis begin compared to how it ends?
2. What is the purpose of the book of Genesis?
3. What is the difference between Genesis 1–11 and Genesis 12–50?
4. How long does it take for the Israelites to possess the land that God promised Abraham?
5. Why is the book of Genesis important to understanding Christian salvation?

Bibliography

Barry, John D., David Bomar, Derek R. Brown, Rachel Klippenstein, Douglas Mangum, Carrie Sinclair Wolcott, Lazarus Wentz, Elliot Ritzema, and Wendy Widder, eds. *The Lexham Bible Dictionary*. Bellingham, WA: Lexham Press, 2016.

Elwell, Walter A. *Evangelical Dictionary of Theology.* 2nd ed. Grand Rapids, MI: Baker Academic, 2004.

Erickson, Millard. *Christian Theology*. 3rd ed. Grand Rapids, MI: Baker Book House, 2013.

Gaebelein, Frank E., ed. *The Expositor's Bible Commentary*, Vol. 2, *Genesis, Exodus, Leviticus, Numbers*. Grand Rapids, MI: Zondervan Publishing House, 1990.

Johnston, Robert D. *Numbers in the Bible: God's Unique Design in Biblical Numbers*. Grand Rapids, MI: Kregel Publications, 1990.

LaSor, William, David Hubbard, and Frederic Bush. *Old Testament Survey: The Message, Form and Background of the Old Testament*. 2nd ed. Grand Rapids, MI: Eerdmans, 1996.

Longman III, Tremper. *How to Read Genesis*. Downers Grove, IL: InterVarsity Press, 2005.

Schaeffer, Francis A. *Genesis in Space and Time*. Downers Grove, IL: InterVarsity Press, 1972.

Walton, John H. *Genesis: The NIV Application Commentary*. Grand Rapids, MI: Zondervan, 2001.

Wenham, Gordon J. *Word Biblical Commentary.* Vol.1, *Genesis 1-15.* Grand Rapids, MI: Zondervan, 1987.

Wenham, Gordon J. *Word Biblical Commentary.* Vol. 2, *Genesis 16-50.* Grand Rapids, MI: Zondervan, 1987.

About the Author

Allison Dee Parkman, MD., MDiv., was born in Akron, Ohio. She graduated from the University of Chicago with her BA in African-American Studies. She earned her medical degree from the Medical College of Ohio (now the College of Medicine and Life Sciences at the University of Toledo). She completed her Family Medicine Residency training at the Baton Rouge General and completed her Urgent Care Fellowship training at the University Hospitals in Cleveland, Ohio. She is a board-certified Family Medicine physician and the Medical Director of FastLane Urgent Care in Zachary, LA with over 15 years of Urgent Care experience.

Dr. Parkman accepted Jesus Christ as her savior, was baptized and filled with the Holy Spirit at First Apostolic Faith Church in Akron, Ohio. Dr. Parkman has been teaching Sunday School for over 20 years. Her desire to help young people gain a better understanding and love for the Bible motivated her to start writing her own lessons. In an effort to continue her education and become a more effective teacher she completed her MDiv from Liberty University in 2018.

Although Dr. Parkman started out teaching middle school students, she has taught students of all ages and levels from pre-k to the adult classes. She served as Superintendent of Christian Education at the Way of Holiness Ministries in Jackson, LA. Dr. Parkman currently resides in Zachary, LA .

www.dradp.com